This story of ‘t [illegible] Russia’ portrays Sergei [illegible] (1895–1925), a leader of Russian Imagism, one of the dominant artistic trends of the 1920s that was notorious for its romantic amoralism and aesthetic provocation. Written by Imagism’s co-founder and Esenin’s best friend, Anatoly Mariengof, this frank and detailed memoir is indispensable for anyone interested in the literary avant-garde of the 1920s.

‘Esenin was a living, vibrant hub of that artistic energy which, to quote Pushkin, we call the highest manifestation of Mozartian talent and the Mozartian element.’ — Boris Pasternak.

Anatoly Mariengof (1897-1962) was well known as a poet, novelist, and dramatist in the 1920s. After *A Novel Without Lies* (1927) which outraged both the authorities and the public at the time, he was hardly ever published, he died in obscurity to be resurrected only in the 1990s.
See his novel *Cynics* in *Glas* One.

Glas New Russian Writing

contemporary Russian literature
in English translation

Volume 23

Back issues of Glas:

REVOLUTION

SOVIET GROTESQUE

WOMEN'S VIEW

LOVE & FEAR

BULGAKOV & MANDELSTAM

JEWS & STRANGERS

BOOKER WINNERS & OTHERS

LOVE RUSSIAN STYLE

THE SCARED GENERATION

BOOKER WINNERS & OTHERS — II

CAPTIVES

BEYOND THE LOOKING-GLAS

A WILL & A WAY

SKUNK: A LIFE by Peter Aleshkovsky

CHILDHOOD

SONECHKA by Ludmila Ulitskaya

THE GRASSY STREET by Asar Eppel

THINGS THAT HAPPENED by Boris Slutsky

THE PORTABLE PLATONOV

THE FACE-MAKER AND THE MUSE by Leonid Latynin

THE NOMADIC SOUL by Irina Muravyova

Anatoly Mariengof

A Novel Without Lies

Translated by Jose Alaniz

EDITORS:
NATASHA PEROVA & ARCH TAIT & JOANNE TURNBULL

Camera-ready copy: Tatiana Shaposhnikova
Front cover: a photograph of Esenin and Mariengof, 1919

GLAS Publishers (Russia)
Moscow 119517, P.O.Box 47, Russia
tel./tax: +7(095)441 9157
e-mail: perova@glas.msk.su

GLAS Publishers (UK)
Dept. of Russian Literature,
University of Birmingham,
Birmingham, B15 2TT, UK
tel/fax: +44(0)121-414 6047
e-mail: a.l.tait@bham.ac.uk

UK and EUROPE
Central Books Ltd.
99 Wallis Road, London E9 5LN, UK
tel: 181-986 4854; fax: 181-533 5821
e-mail: orders@centralbooks.com

USA and Canada
Ivan R. Dee
1332 North Halsted St., Chicago,
Illinois 60622-2694, USA
tel: 1-312-787 6262; fax: 1-312-787 6269
toll-free: +1-800-462-6420
e-mail: elephant@ivanrdee.com

WORLD WIDE WEB:
http://www.bham.ac.uk/glas

ISBN 5-7172-0049-8

Printed at the 'Novosti' printing press, Moscow

THE LAST POET OF WOODEN RUSSIA

Anatoly Mariengof's *A Novel Without Lies* is neither a novel nor a memoir in the traditional sense. Rather it is a mosaic of very personal memories of a very close friend, who happened to be a great poet. Sergei Esenin burst into Mariengof's life in the summer of 1918. Soon the two would be sharing a room, and even a bed (to keep warm) in unheated, post-revolutionary Moscow while dedicating poems to each other, running a bookshop, and arriving at the principles of Imagism. Their legendary friendship — 'great, beautiful, steadfast and seemingly indissoluble', in the words of Mariengof — lasted until Esenin's suicide in 1925.

Here Mariengof traces the arc of Esenin's poetic career against the flamboyant background of bohemian Moscow before and after the Revolution. In those years of fantastic upheaval, so destructive to the ordinary man and so stimulating to the creative mind, successive new literary schools rose up and reacted against one another. Thus the mystic and impressionistic Symbolism (1896-1910) of Bely and Blok gave way to the concise and concrete Acmeism (1910-1917) of Akhmatova and Mandelstam; while the iconoclastic and sound-driven Futurism (1912-1927) of Mayakovsky and Khlebnikov was attacked by the founders of Imagism (1919-27), Vadim Shershenevich, Esenin and Mariengof. Although Russian Imagists were aware of Ezra Pound and English Imagism and they also opposed Symbolism, the links between them are very tenuous.

Sergei Esenin (1895-1925) was born into a family of Old Believers in Konstantinovo on the Oka River, Ryazan Province. In 1911, he left his village for Moscow where he won instant fame with his lyrical peasant verse. He was hailed as 'the last poet of wooden Russia' and as a true 'people's poet'. Esenin embraced the Revolution of 1917 as a social and spiritual transformation that would give the Russian peasant the land he needed.

Esenin's first collection of poems, *Radunitsa* (1915), celebrated religious Russia and the village of his childhood. His next book, *Otherland*, glorified the utopian view of peasant values as an antidote to urban industrialization. In 1920, he wrote *Pugachev*, a drama about the 18th-century peasant revolutionary. And almost every day he wrote one or two poems. To Esenin, his life in every detail — the girl with Biblical eyes, the foolhardy foal, the night in jail, etc. — was first and foremost grist for his poetry.

In January 1919, Esenin, Mariengof and Shershenevich published their Imagist manifesto advocating a poetry of unusual and arresting images. For three years (1922-24) they published a journal, *Inn for Travelers in the Beautiful.* Esenin, meanwhile, was turning to the provocative verse of his *Confessions of a Hooligan* and *Moscow of the Taverns.* His work now tended to self-deprecation; it hinted both at his remorse at not having fulfilled his messianic role as a people's poet and at his disillusionment with Bolshevik Russia.

In 1922 Esenin married the much older American dancer Isadora Duncan. Their brief and tempestuous union was spent mostly travelling through Europe (where 'nobody cares about poetry') and the United States, where Esenin was known only as 'Isadora's young Russian husband.' Esenin did not like the West, at the same time he dreaded Soviet Russia. 'It makes me sick that I, a legitimate Russian son, should be treated like a bastard in my own country,' he wrote to his old Imagist friend Alexander Kusikov in 1923. 'I'm fed up with this whorish condescension of the powers that be.' The increasingly unstable and alcoholic Esenin returned to Russia alone.

His first wife was Zinaida Raikh (later she married the great stage director Vsevolod Meyerhold who made a famous actress out of her and raised Esenin's two children by her). His third wife was Sofya Tolstoy, Lev Tolstoy's granddaughter, whom he married shortly before his suicide, in September 1925. Obviously he was not happy with her either, complaining of the oppressive presence of the Great Old Man's spirit in the house.

Upon his return from abroad Esenin parted company with the Imagists. And on 28 December 1925, in a desolate hotel room in Leningrad, he hung himself, having written his last poem in his own blood.

Anatoly Mariengof (1897-1962) is the author of *Cynics* (see *Glas* One), an actual novel set in Moscow during the years of War Communism and Lenin's New Economic Policy. A time — despite the hunger, cold, and communist terror — of youthful passions and great hope. Writes Mariengof: 'It was an interesting age, young, spirited, eventful and philosophical.'

Mariengof and Esenin remained inseparable until 1922 when Mariengof married the actress Anna Nikritina and Esenin married Isadora Duncan. In *A Novel Without Lies*, Mariengof set out to paint an unvarnished portrait of his old friend. And he succeeded.

Regarding the accuracy of his facts Mariengof wrote: *'Whatever devilish memory one might possess one is unable to remember verbatim all the words and phrases said several decades ago. But the essence and meaning of the dialogues in my book are all true in spirit if not in wording. Such is human memory.'*

First published in 1927, the book was soon banned as an insult to the 'people's poet'. It was reprinted only in 1988.

THE EDITORS

More on Esenin and Mariengof:

Gordon McVay, *Esenin: a Life*, 1976;
Isadora and Esenin: The Story of Isadora Duncan and Sergei Esenin. 1980

Sergei Esenin, *Confessions of a Hooligan: Fifty Poems.* Translated by Geoffrey Thursley. 1973

Anatoly Mariengof, *Cynics*, a novel. Translated by Andrew Bromfield. *Glas* #1

Мариенгоф.

A Novel Without Lies

1

Penza, a city in Central Russia where Mariengof spent his youth.

I had a friend in Penza: an eccentric fellow. The first time I saw him he wore celluloid cuffs, tinkling like armor from under his gray school jacket, a black-rimmed pince-nez on a thick cord, and long poet's hair, dangling like fat black icicles onto a shiny celluloid collar.

Nizhny Novgorod, a city on the Volga.

At the time I had just been transferred from the Nizhny Novgorod Nobles' Institute to the grammar school in Penza.

Our morals at the institute were strict — we'd never dream of wearing long poet's hair. If you neglected to drop by the barber for a week or two the headmaster would confront you in the corridor or on the pinkish marble staircase. He was a ridiculous man — a Czech (who pronounced the soft L as hard, and the hard one as soft). He always said the same thing:

'The ancient Greeks lliked their hair llong for the sake of beauty, whil'e the Scythians wore it llong in order to terrify their foes. And you, l'ittlle boy, why do you wear it llong?'

It was a difficult thing, at our institute, to cultivate a penchant for poetry and be a favorite of the muses.

Seeing Zhenya Litvinov with his celluloid cuffs and

poetic head of hair I understood that here my gift for verse was fated to blossom.

Zhenya also had a passion for literature — a remarkable passion, after his own peculiar manner. He wrote no verse or short stories, read few books, but subscribed to practically all the thick and thin journals from Moscow, to the literary anthologies and collections, poetry and prose, harboring a special devotion to Scorpio and Musagette, the most elegant and fashionable of the capital's publishers at the time. Everything he received from Moscow he laid out on the shelves, unopened. I would drop by, open the books, read them — and for this he regarded me with gratitude and friendship.

'Thick journals' — this is how Russians call traditional literary journals

Scorpio and Musagette (headed by Andrei Bely [1880-1934], a major Symbolist poet) were two leading publishing houses specializing in Russian Symbolists and Western Modernists.

It was Zhenya Litvinov who introduced me to the poetry of Sergei Esenin. In the summer of 1918, four years after my arrival in Penza. I had finished school, served on the German front and recently returned to Penza in the loo of a first class train car. I spent 96 hours, fighting sleep on the toilet seat, arousing the envy of my carriage-mates who like me were fleeing the field of glory. Zhenya was amused by politics (as he had been, in his time, by literature), he subscribed to virtually all the newspapers published in Moscow and Petrograd. The leftist *Banner of Labor* had just published Alexander Blok's *The Scythians* and *The Twelve*, and Sergei Esenin's *Transfiguration* and *Otherland.*

This was the era when Esenin's 'clouds barked,' when his 'gold-toothed summit roared,' his Virgin walked along with a switch, 'calling the calves to paradise,' and, like his Ryazan cow, he addressed God, proposing 'to deliver.'

Overjoyed by his verse, the power of his words and his riotous peasant wit, I tried to picture him in my mind's eye. I had an image of a peasant, about 35, over six feet tall, with a beard like a salver of red copper.

Three months later I met Esenin in Moscow.

But I want to make a one last mention of Zhenya Litvinov.

Early in 1920 I saw him on Kuznetsky Most Street. He had just arrived in Moscow from Penza with three dozen silver soupspoons. These spoons were all that remained of his once not inconsiderable property. He was the son of a merchant: their two-story stone house stood on Sennaya Square, and in it they had had every comfort in abundance.

Zhenya came to Moscow for glory. In what field glory was supposed to come to him — that he didn't know. He obviously believed that in Moscow glory rained down on Penzans from out of the blue.

Every day, anticipating glory, Zhenya Litvinov sold a soupspoon. The last time I saw him was almost a month after his ill-fated arrival in Moscow. He had six silver spoons left, and glory had not shown up. He spent four more days in the capital. With his last two spoons he bought a return ticket to Penza.

I never saw him again. My dear Penza! My dear Penzans!

2

The first few weeks in Moscow I lived with my cousin Boris (known as Bob), at the Second House of Soviets (located in the hotel Metropol) and I was bursting with unwonted pride. No wonder: on the sidewalk, at the entrance, stood a rifle-bearing sailor; in the hall, a Red Guard with a Browning handed out passes which were collected by two Red Guards with machine-gun cartridge belts slung over their shoulders. I must confess I was even a bit let down when tea was brought to the room by a meek creature in a white lace apron.

Around midnight, when I was just about to draw a blanket over my head, into the room ran a small, light person with light eyes, light hair and light beard resembling the little corner of a canvas table cloth. His eyes danced cheerfully. In a word, I liked him very much.

Running into the room, this light man bumped into a pile of books. Imprinted on the top specimen's cover, in a thick black script, was the title *Exodus* and a picture of some beast-like creature (not quite on two feet, not quite on four), making away into the diaphanous distance with a rose like a head of red cabbage in its blue paws. The artist had been asked to reflect on the world war, as well as the February and October revolutions.

The Great October Socialist Revolution of 1917 was preceded by the February 1917 bourgeois revolution which overthrew the monarchy.

The mysterious fellow opened the book and read out loud:

Beloved,
Be a scapegoat today
Of my tenderness.

Those three lines were called a poem, and the idea lodged within them was supposed to surpass in authenticity and artistic force all representations of love generated by world literature up to the present time. At least, so the author hoped.

To my indignation the stranger exploded with the tactless laughter, instantly revealing himself as a person who gave not a thought to the arts.

And to top it off, holding his tummy he exclaimed:

'Amazing... Never in my life have I read such nonsense!'

At this point Bob, jabbing a finger in my direction, said:

'Well, here's the author.'

The stranger amicably put out his hand.

When, some ten minutes later, he left the room, taking with him a copy of the first Imagist anthology (published in Penza) as a memento, I asked Boris, twitching with rage:

'Who was that idiot?'

'Bukharin!' Bob answered, spreading the butter I'd brought from Penza onto a slice of rye bread.

Nikolai Bukharin (1888-1938), Communist Party leader. Held various important positions. Executed as 'enemy of the people.'

That night my fate was decided. Two days later I was sitting at a large desk as the executive literary secretary of the Central Executive Committee press, at the corner of Tverskaya and Mokhovaya streets.

It was a warm August day. My desk at the press stood near the window. Along the street, a squadron of Latvian Riflemen marched in even, stone-like ranks. Their overcoats seemed made not from gray soldier's cloth, but from steel. At their head they carried a banner declaring: 'We demand mass terror!'

Latvian Riflemen, a division during the First World War which later took part in the October Revolution of 1917 and the Civil War on the side of the Bolsheviks.

Someone lightly touched me on the shoulder.

'Excuse me, comrade. May I see the press director, comrade Eremeyev?'

Before me stood a small chap in a blue *poddyovka*.

Beneath the *poddyovka* he wore a white silk shirt. His hair was wavy, blond, with a golden shimmer. A large curl fell seemingly carelessly (but in fact quite intentionally) on his forehead. The curl gave him the air of a young and pretty hairdresser from the provinces. And only the blue eyes (not too large and not too pretty) made his face more intelligent despite the curl, and the blue *poddyovka*, and his silk shirt collar, embroidered like a Russian towel.

Poddyovka — a tight-fitting peasant coat.

'Tell comrade Eremeyev that Sergei Esenin is here.'

3

I was renting a room (with my classmate Molabukh) on Petrovka Street, in the apartment of an engineer.

He had let the room to us fearing that part of his apartment might be confiscated together with his gilt furniture with its worn plush, his massive bronze candelabras and portraits of his 'ancestors' — as we took to calling the engineer's parents — which hung on the walls in heavy frames.

In the early post-revolutionary years of economic dislocation, most of the private residences were expropriated and turned into communal apartments. Their former owners were allowed to keep one room for themselves.

We did not live up to the engineer's hopes. The very next day after moving in we yanked the fly-blown 'ancestors' off the walls, piled them up in a big heap and carried them off to the kitchen.

After such a Bolshevik operation the engineer's grandmother suspected us of being secret government agents and started putting her ancient ear to our keyhole.

That's when we took it into our heads to shrink the remaining stock of her earthly days.

The vehicle we came up with for this mission would

have shocked, in its refinement, the perspicacious mind of the founder of the Jesuit order.

Lounging on the plush sofa whose back bordered the keyhole, we would blandly engage in more or less the following conversation:

'What do you think, Misha: grandma's bronze "candlelabras," do they weigh about two poods?'

A pood is about 40 pounds or 16 kg.

'Sure.'

'Do you happen to know what century they are?'

'18th, grandma says.'

'And supposedly they're by a famous Italian master?'

'Florentine.'

'I'm thinking, if we dragged 'em over to Sukharevka, they'd fork over five poods of wheat for 'em.'

Sukharevka, the biggest flea market in Moscow.

'Sure.'

'So, let 'em stay here 'til Sunday, then we'll take 'em.'

'Sure.'

At that moment, on the other side of the wall, something plumped down, moaned dolefully and shuffled its shoes in despair.

And on Monday we'd start it all over again.

Before long we even got ourselves an accomplice in this vile business.

Vadim Shershenevich and Ryurik Ivnev started hanging around our place on Petrovka. We were discussing a new poetic school of the image.

Vadim Shershenevich (1893-1942) poet, one of the founders and the main theoretician of Russian Imagism.

Ryurik Ivnev (pseudonym of Mikhail Kovalev, 1891-1975) poet, one of the founders of Imagism.

Several times at the press I had traded ideas on this subject with Esenin.

At last we agreed to meet and talk, and, if we saw eye to eye in our understanding and definition of the image, to work out a manifesto.

Esenin was the last to show up, over an hour late. He came in, out of breath, wiping the sweat from his brow with a blue-bordered handkerchief. He'd been running up and down Dmitrovka Street instead of Petrovka, looking for a building with our number on it. But on Dmitrovka there was only a vacant lot at that number; he ran around the lot, got angry and decided that all this had been done on purpose to elude him, to work out the manifesto without him and afterwards have a laugh at his expense.

Russian Imagism advocated poetry based on a series of arresting and unusual images. Although Russian Imagists were aware of Ezra Pound and English Imagism and opposed to Symbolism, the links between them are very tenuous.

Esenin had always had a pathological mistrust of others. Enemies, their dirty tricks and rumors about him — all this he invented out of thin air.

He loved the *muzhik* in himself and bore him proudly. But during his bouts of hypochondria he always suspected us of superior smiles and our words of secret meanings. All this, of course, was complete nonsense; he bristled for nothing.

Late into the night we'd drink tea with saccharine, talk about the image and its place in poetry, of the rebirth of great literature such as *Song of Songs*, *The Kalevala* and *The Lay of Prince Igor's Campaign*.

Muzhik — peasant, villager, often used as a synonym for 'real man.'

Esenin had his own classification of images. The static ones he called 'illuminations', the active, dynamic ones, 'ship-like', the latter incomparably superior to the former. He spoke of the ornamental design of the Russian alphabet; of the imagistic symbolism in the everyday; of the peak gables shaped as horses on peasant houses, bearing them away, like a carriage, into the sky; of the patterns on fabrics; of the images in riddles, proverbs and contemporary ditties.

Esenin needed formal schooling, and not only he. In our impoverished state of mind we could have done with some ourselves.

One savvy writer, responding to the question, 'What is culture?' recounted the following moralistic tale:

'A rich American arrived in England. He traveled throughout the country and was surprised by nothing. The purchasing power of the dollar had made a skeptic out of him. And only once, struck by the unusual lawn in the ancestral park of an English aristocrat, did he ask of the gardener how he could achieve such a lawn back home.

"Nothing simpler," says the gardener. "Plow, sow, and when it shoots up, mow it twice a week and water it twice a day. If you do that, in three hundred years you'll have a lawn just like this one." '

All of Russian literature is just a bit more than a century old. We write prose well, when we're translating from French.

We should feel overjoyed, not grumble, when a writer learns form.

Before we dispersed, Esenin read his verses. Maybe because he shouted, setting the pendants on our 'candelabras' tinkling, and proclaimed himself now the goose who laid the golden literary egg, now the prophet Sergei; or maybe because of the words themselves, sturdy and coarse — on the other side of the wall, where grandma was resting her bones, something sobbed, groaned and shuffled its slippers despairingly all the way to the water closet.

4

Every day, around two o'clock, Esenin would walk into the press, sit next to me, and place a yellow packet of pickled cucumbers on my desk piled high with manuscripts.

Rivulets of brine flowed from the packet onto the desk.

The cucumbers' green flesh crunched in his teeth, and the salty juice oozed out, spreading in violet patches over manuscript pages.

Esenin lectured:

'You can't enter Russian literature just like that, off the cuff. You've got to conduct a skillful game and the subtlest policy.'

He jabbed his finger at me:

'It'll be hard for you, Tolya, in patent-leather shoes and with that perfect part, every hair in place. How can you get by without poetical distraction? Do poets really live in a cloud in iron-pressed trousers? Who's going to believe that? Look at Andrei Bely. His hair's already gray and he's got a bald patch the size of Wolf's one-volume Pushkin, and even in front of his own cook, who washes his underpants, he walks around showing off his poetic inspiration. It doesn't hurt to play the fool. They so love a little nitwit here. Everybody's got to find his own satisfaction. You know how I climbed Parnassus?'

Tolya is a diminutive of Anatoly.

Esenin burst into boyish laughter.

'This is where the matter should have been carried out shrewdly. Let each one of them think, "I introduced him to Russian literature." It's flattering for them, and I don't care. Gorodetsky thinks he introduced me? Sure.

Sergei Gorodetsky (1884-1967) poet, adherent of Acmeism.

Nikolai Klyuev (1887-1937) a peasant poet. Widely known at the time. His verse contains elements of mysticism and Symbolism and strong folkloric motifs. Esenin had a 'love-hate' relationship with Klyuev throughout his life. Klyuev was executed as an 'enemy of the people.'

Dmitry Merezhkovsky (1866-1941) and Zinaida Hippius (1869-1945), husband and wife, were both writers and critics, leaders of the decadent trend in art. They emigrated in 1920.

Klyuev introduced me? Sure. Sologub and Chebotarevskaya brought me in? Sure they did. Even Merezhkovsky with his Madame Hippius, and Blok, and Ryurik Ivnev. It's true that Ivnev was the first poet I went to — he squinted his lorgnette at me, I remember, and before I had managed to read even a dozen lines already he was saying in his thin little voice, "Ach, how amazing! Ach, what genius! Ach ..." and seizing me by the hand he dragged me from big name to big name, lavishing his "achs." While I, you might say, blushed like a girl at every injection of praise and didn't look anybody in the eye, out of shyness. What fun!'

Esenin smiled. He looked at his laced-up American boots (by then he had managed to part forever with his *poddyovka*, his shirt embroidered like a towel, and his accordion-like high boots) and quite sincerely (not with manufactured sincerity, of which he also was a master) said:

'You know, I had never in my life worn those village boots and that bedraggled *poddyovka* in which I appeared before them. I told them that I was going to Riga to roll barrels. There was nothing to eat, I said. But I'd go to Petersburg just for a day or two, while my party of stevedores made it big. Barrels — ha! I came to Petersburg for worldwide fame, for a bronze monument... Klyuev here's the same. He pretended to be a house-painter. He came into Gorodetsky's kitchen through the back entrance: "Would you happen to need something painted?" And here we go, he starts reading verses to the cook. You know what poets' cooks are. She dashed straight to the master of the house. The lord shows up. He calls him into the rooms, Klyuev doesn't come. "And me soiling up the lord's armchair, and tracking up his floor!" The master proposes they have a seat. Klyuev deliberates: "Now, we'll stand up..." And so, standing before the master in the kitchen, he read his verses.'

Esenin was quiet for a moment. His eyes turned from blue to a furious gray. His eyelashes reddened — as if someone had threaded them with a scarlet thread along the edges:

'Well, and then they hauled me through the salons for about three weeks, to warble my way through bawdy ditties to the accompaniment of an accordion. They'd ask me to read a couple of poems for show. I'd read two or three — they'd hide their yawns in a fist, and then I'd belt out profanity all night long... God, how I hate all these Sologubs and Hippiuses!'

His eyes reverted to blue. The cucumber crunched in his teeth. A tiny green drop of brine fell onto a manuscript. Wiping the cucumber tear from the page with his sleeve, he added in a heated voice:

'Out of all the Petersburg crowd I like only Razumnik and Sergei Gorodetsky. Even though his Nymph (that's what they called Gorodetsky's wife) would make me start up the samovar and send me to the local shop for thread.'

5

On Tverskaya, not far from Gazetny Lane, the actors of the 'Moscow Farce' theater organized a canteen.

Strictly speaking — not in today's parlance but in

Alexander Blok (1880-1921) a major Russian poet, a leader of Russian Symbolism. First he embraced the Revolution, but soon was disillusioned with the new regime.

Fyodor Sologub (1863-1927) Symbolist writer, author of *The Petty Demon*.

Razumnik Ivanov (1878-1946), known as Ivanov-Razumnik, critic, historian, philosopher. Arrested in 1933.

the dear naive notions of 1919 — we would have to call that dim, crooked little corridor furnished with three-legged tables (from some antediluvian beer joint that once prospered near Korovy Val Street) not a disparaging name like 'canteen', but an absolutely, no-doubt-about-it first-rate restaurant.

NEP — New Economic Policy, a period of state-controlled private enterprise which replaced War Communism and lasted from 1921 to the mid-1930s.

Before the primogenitor of these NEP establishments, Esenin and I would eat in a miserable little basement, worth describing here: a cook in a halo of red hair (like a saint from an old Novgorodian icon); a red-brick stove the size of an Empire-style bed; unpainted kitchen tables, wooden spoons, and ... plates from a royal service with two-headed gold eagles on them.

The red-haired cook would turn any indigestible carrion into more or less decent pilafs, sroganoffs and entrecotes.

A most improbable phantasmagoria.

We ate and wept — from the dizzying fumes, the smoke and the stench.

Esenin said:

'I can't bear it anymore. The whole phantasmagoria's gone to my stomach.'

So we decided to move from the miserable little Hoffmanesque basement to the 'Moscow Farce' canteen.

We went there till the spring, drank brown slops with saccharine and ate tender foal's meat.

Esenin wore a short fur jacket and ridiculous black overshoes that made squelching sounds and scrubbed the ground. You looked at his feet — a man of a respectable age. Nothing ages you more than our Russian galoshes. Get yourself into some galoshes and it's as if you've put on weight and grown confident in disposition.

In our little restaurant, for every mere mortal there were a half-dozen famous writers.

The conversations revolved around poetic imagery and Imagism. The manifesto signed by Esenin, Vadim Shershenevich, Ryurik Ivnev, Georgy Yakulov and myself had just appeared in *The Soviet Land* newspaper.

The Austrian foreign minister Ottokar Chernin relates in his witty memoirs a conversation with Ioffe in Brest-Litovsk at the time of the peace negotiations:

'In the event that the revolution in Russia meets with success (said Emperor Charles' diplomat), Europe will not hesitate to ally herself to Russia's cast of mind. But for now the greatest skepticism is appropriate, and this is why I categorically forbid any meddling in the internal affairs of our country.'

'Mr. Ioffe looked at me with his gentle eyes,' — writes Chernin further on, — 'and then said in a friendly and almost pleading tone:

"All the same I hope we will succeed in bringing forth the revolution in your country as well." '

Esenin had the same manner of looking gently and speaking in an almost pleading tone.

Following one of our conversations on Imagism, when Pimen Karpov had sputtered like a sulfur match lighted on the sole of a shoe, while Pyotr Oreshin had spared neither our parents, nor the soul, nor God, Esenin said after walking a block in silence:

'Some miserable lives they've had ... Oreshin slept in coffins ... Pimen chewed on his jealousy for some ten

Vadim Shershenevich and Ryurik Ivnev, see p. 13

Georgy Yakulov (1884-1928) avant-garde artist, one of the ideologists of Imagism.

Adolf Ioffe (1883-1927) Soviet diplomat, was persecuted as Trotsky's associate, committed suicide.

Pimen Karpov (1884-1963) writer.

Pyotr Oreshin (1887-1938) peasant poet, activist in the Proletkult (Union of Proletarian Culture). Executed as an 'enemy of the people.'

years. Well, they've become like dogs who've had their tails chopped off, so they'll bite people in the haunches.'

The air in our room was fresh, ice-cold.

Esenin grew vicious:

'Their teeny little talents aren't worth five measly kopecks. Just you remember, Anatoly, they'll be licking my boots before long. Sucking up to me, that's what.'

That very winter Nikolai Klyuev himself sent Esenin a letter.

A smooth-tongued letter, all treacle and balm. But Klyuev's syrup held poison — Pimen's poison and Oreshin's bile were no match for Klyuev's.

Esenin read and reread the letter. By evening he knew it backwards and forwards. He yellowed, fell silent, knit his brows, and gathered the skin of his forehead into an accordion.

Then he spent some three days writing a response, with difficulty and great thought, as if composing verse. He would hone a phrase, turning it this way and that, like a Tbilisi inn-keeper turning lamb shashlik over a fire. He dredged out of the innermost recesses of his memory the very things that would make 'Nicky' jaundiced, just like 'Nicky's bright falcon' himself.

Esenin meant to be the leading voice of Russian poetry, and here Klyuev had sent him the 'edifying' advice and praise of a 'foster parent.'

For a long time yet, out of habit, the critics would add fuel to the fire by praising Esenin as 'Klyuev's younger brother.' But Esenin was already standing firmly on his own feet in literature; he spoke in his own voice and wore his own Esenin 'shirt' (as he liked to call the verse form).

After one such review, Esenin ran over to the press to dismantle the typesetting of the old poem with these two lines:

The gentle apostle Klyuev
Carried us all in his arms.

But he was too late. The machine had already spit out its final sheets.

6

More about Esenin's treatment of people.

During the years of War Communism, we, the Imagists, had our own press and a small bookshop with a cafe, Pegasus' Stall.

War Communism (1917-21) a period of all-round nationalization, state monopoly on trade, redivision of the land and property, and requisitioning of all 'surplus' goods.

For this reason we ran around quite a bit to various institutions, people's commissions, and the Moscow City Council.

I'll speak about the press, the bookshop and Pegasus' Stall in more detail below — like it or not, quite a few of our days, thoughts, joys and sorrows are linked with them.

But now I want to tack on a few more nuances, a few more specks — not blotches, but not lies either. Only a cold stranger's hand will prefer whitewash and rouge to other hues.

'Treatment' — what a good little word.

Esenin always loved to turn a word inside out, to arrive at its original meaning.

Words, in their centuries-old wanderings, tend to

wear out. With our tongues we've licked clean the beauteous metaphorical figures of some, the aural image of others, and the sense, subtle and sarcastic, of still more.

Perhaps it was by carefully listening to the inner core of every word that Esenin came to the conclusion that man must be 'treated.'

In those years the director of the Central Press, Tsentropechat, was a marvelous man, Boris Fyodorovich Malkin. Before the revolution he had edited a small opposition newspaper in Penza, *Black Earth.* I recall he showed great kindness to me when I brought him a notebook of my verse.

The wellbeing of our press depended on Tsentropechat. Malkin was the chief wholesale purchaser.

Once we were sitting in his office. Esenin was fiddling with an order in his hands — we needed the director's signature on it. By then, our books and we ourselves had become a pain in the neck for Malkin. The very word 'Imagist' set people on edge.

Malkin glances at us with his tender sad eyes (the only kind I ever saw on him) and, getting distracted, he tells us something about his Tsentropechat business. Esenin nods in assent and goes into raptures. The more Malkin talks, the more Esenin revels. And, finally, with the greatest cunning, in feigned admiration of Malkin's administrative genius, he exclaims:

'You know, Boris Fyodorovich, they will, I submit, bestow a medal on you for this!'

One Eseninesque word like that and the kindly Malkin becomes even kindlier. As a matter of fact no medals existed at that time.

And just look at that — the order's signed for another six months.

Esenin, meanwhile, having noted the naive fascination with his just-invented medal, was already secreting it away in his memory against a similar situation later on. And, since such situations, thanks to our numerous projects came up often, the distribution of Esenin's medals proceeded apace.

Some four weeks after that, as we were leaving Malkin's office, I said angrily to him:

'Do me a favor, Sergei — drop your medals. That's the third one you've "bestowed" on Malkin this month, you know.'

Esenin raised a brow:

'Leave me alone! Don't tell me my business.'

His face was made handsome by dark eyebrows; they suggested a bird split in half, one wing to each side. When he frowned in anger, the cloven fowl would bring together its wings, otherwise spread wide.

And when we had to go to the Moscow City Council to receive a permit to open a bookshop, Esenin spoke to Lev Borisovich Kamenev in Klyuev's Olonets accent, rounding his O's and using familiar language like muzhiks:

'Would ye be sO kind, daddy dear, Lev BOrisOvich, an' done dO this fer us.'

Lev Kamenev (1883-1936) real name Rozenfeld, Lenin's associate in the 1917 Revolution, held a number of important positions in the Communist Party and the government.

Olonets, a town on Lake Ladoga in the north of Russia

7

With a heaving sigh from the very bottom of his stomach, Esenin looked upon his father, mother and sisters (living in the village of Konstantinovo, in the Ryazan province), as a heavy burden.

He sent little money to the village, always grudgingly, always with anger and grumbling. Never on his own initiative, either, but only after insistent letters, outcries and inducements.

From time to time his father would come in from the country. He spoke timorously of want, of crop failure, bad potatoes, rotted hay. He twirled his thin little hemp-colored beard, and wiped his teary red eyes with a filthy little rag. Esenin listened skeptically to his father's speeches. He reminded him of the rainy summer and hot sunny days at the time of the hay-mowing; of the good potato harvest everywhere else; of the generally decent harvest in the Ryazan province. The more he remembered, the angrier he got:

'You don't want to do anything back there, and I'm like your purse. When I kick the bucket you'll cry over the purse, not me.'

He produced a book from under a pillow and in a fit of temper read out loud about a profiteer who got his foot lopped off by a locomotive. They were carrying him to the casualty ward, blood gushing everywhere — a ghastly business — and the whole time he's pleading to have them find his foot; all he's worried about is the twenty rubles hidden in the boot on the severed member.

'You're all like that back there.'

His father wiped his tearful red eyes with the soiled rag and tugged at his sparse bast-like beard. In the end Esenin produced the money and showed the old man the door.

Each time after his father's departure, he'd start deliberating what to do about his sisters, whether he should bring them to Moscow to study or not. He was inclined to wait, and maybe leave them in the country for good. He struggled to convince himself of this in accordance with his scruples. He concocted arguments that he himself didn't believe in. He invoked the philosophy of Hamsun's 'Landowner' about the happiness in nature and on the land; there's little joy, he said, in fluttering your skirts along the sidewalks and having abortions.

'Better to leave them to clean out cow sheds and have babies.'

He himself thoroughly enjoyed the city and city life with its worn-down and bespittled sidewalks. In the four years we lived together he made it back to his Konstantinovo a grand total of one time. He meant to stay there about ten days, but came scampering back in disgust after three, grousing and saying that by the morning of the second day he didn't know what to do with himself, he was bored to tears.

He did not want to bring his sisters to the city lest the 'young misses' vulgarize his tropes. What a superb contrast his sisters' homespun coats and flowery chintz kerchiefs, his father's gnarled plow and his mother's milk pail must have made for the top hat, tuxedo and black cloak he aspired to then!

8

I remember a fire in Nizhny Novgorod. The houses along a steep slope were burning. It looked like the little houses were turning somersaults. Under the clay heel of the slope, in a smelly, filthy gully, was Baltchug: stalls, little shops, stores with all manner of junk. Big passions and petty trade.

When the slope blazed up and the wind raised red dust in clouds and carried it towards Baltchug, a huge black crowd gawked at the flames and shuddered. Nearby stood a man, almost a head taller than the flat, black wall of people. A gray hat, a light gray suit, yellow gloves and yellow lacquered shoes lent him the air of a foreigner. But the eyes, the mouth and the shaven, softly rounded cheekbones were native, Nizhegorodian. No English material, no gloves — even the yellowest in the world — could fool anybody there.

He stood there, like a monument of gray cast-iron. And he gazed upon the fire monumentally, looking down on it from above. Then he removed his hat and put his hands behind his back. To my eye he looked just like the cast-iron Pushkin on Tverskoy Boulevard.

Suddenly, someone whispered his name. It flashed through the crowd. And he, who vied with cast-iron, now vied with the flames for attention.

The people turned away from the fire, started looking into his eyes unceremoniously, jabbing their fingers in his direction and whispering to one other.

Several hours later I ran across my monument on Pokrovka Street, the main thoroughfare in Nizhny Novgorod. I followed him along the opposite side of the street, never taking my eyes off the man. Later, for some three months straight, I wrote about five poems a day, just to draw a bit closer to a future of great fame and not die of anticipation — awaiting the day when others would start pointing their unceremonious fingers at me.

Many years passed.

I was running hand in hand with Esenin along Kuznetsky Most Street.

All of a sudden I saw him. He was standing by a motor car. Again a very good suit, very nice hat and beautiful gloves. Again looking like a foreigner despite his Nizhegorodian eyes and our native shaven, softly-rounded high cheekbones.

'It's good that monuments don't age!' I mused.

In the same way passers-by pointed at him, looked under the hat and murmured:

'Chaliapin.'

Fyodor Chaliapin (1873-1938) Russian bass singer. Emigrated in 1922.

I could feel Esenin's hand quivering with excitement. His pupils widened. A blush erupted on his dull-yellow cheeks from the thrill. He forced out of himself, in a voice choked with envy, with resentment, with rapture:

'Now that is glory!'

And it was then that I understood Esenin would sacrifice anything, even his life, to achieve this silly, this wonderful, this terrible fame.

And so it was.

Several months later we took a ride in a car — Esenin, the sculptor Sergei Konyonkov and I.

Sergei Konyonkov (1874-1971) a major Russian sculptor working with marble and wood.

Konyonkov proposed that we go pick up the young Chaliapin girls (Chaliapin himself was living abroad by then). Esenin was delighted at the suggestion.

We dropped by. Esenin seated a homely freckled girl next to him in the car. The whole way he spoke affectionate words and gazed at her tenderly.

We arrived home tired and worn out — we'd been driving over terrible roads outside Moscow for some

Mikhail Molabukh (real name Grigory Kolobov). Chief of the Transport Department at the Soviet Economic Council.

five hours. That evening Esenin sat next to me on the bed, put an arm about my neck, and whispered into my ear:

'Listen, Tolya — it'd be splendid, wouldn't it: Esenin and Chaliapina... Hm? Should I perhaps get married?'

9

Alexander Kusikov (1896-1977, real name Sandro Beibulet Ku: a Chechen by nationality he Russified his name), Imagist poet. Emigrated to Paris in 1925.

It so happened that in the spring of 1919 Esenin and I found ourselves without a place to live. We camped at friends' (men and women), in an indescribable room at the Europa Hotel, in Molabukh's coach, in short: anywhere, anytime and anyhow.

Once we split up for the night. Esenin went to Kusikov's on the Arbat, and I made my bed on a small sofa in the office of the then famous and inimitable Poets' Cafe.

This 'cradle of glory' was located on Tverskaya, not far from Kamergersky Lane.

Poets' Cafe, functioning as a writers' club, existed from 1919 to 1925 at 18 Tverskaya St., formerly the Cafe Domino whose owner fled Russia during the Revolution.

The wet nurse who coddled this large family of subsequently scandalous and celebrated poets was a big-faced Siberian cardsharp and bartender the size of a kiosk named Afanasy Nesterenko.

When professor Kogan delivered his two-hour lectures on revolutionary poetry, lulling the pallorous young misses in white gauze aprons and the shock-headed, wide-eyed Red Army soldiers with their gloomy lady friends from (by now deserted) Tverskaya; when even the merry and risque inscriptions on the wall had grown drowsy, along with Vasily Kamensky's faded and hole-ridden boot hanging from the ceiling — that was when Nesterenko would approach us and, resting his lion-like paw on a shoulder, ask:

'Comrade poets, you know who our lecturer is today?'

Fearfully looking our red-mugged benefactor in the eye we whispered:

'Professor Kogan.'

In response to which Nesterenko thundered:

'Not Kogan, sir, but Afanasy Nesterenko, yes sir. From your own pockets you'll see that, sir.'

On days like that we got no free dinner.

But let's get back to the story.

Esenin and I decided that the next morning he would come by and we'd go to a friend's dacha outside Moscow. The sun woke me up early. It was a gorgeous spring day. I wiped my eyes and reached out for the watch on the chair. No watch ... I started fumbling for it under the sofa, under the chair, under the headboard...

'Filched!'

I remembered that in my wallet I had enough money for five or six meals — a fair sum.

I panicked. No wallet either.

'Those bastards!'

I wanted to get up — my boots had vanished...

I thought of pulling on my pants — alas, there was nothing to pull on.

And so in the space of some three minutes I discovered one loss after another: my watch ... wallet ... boots ... trousers ... jacket, socks, tie...

The most amusing thing was the progressive nature of the discoveries and alternating degrees of shock.

Vasily Kamensky (1884-1961), a Futurist poet.

Pyotr Kogan (1872-1932) literary historian, author of books on Esenin and on proletarian poets.

Had it not been for Esenin, I would have had to sit there until four in the afternoon, in my birthday suit, inside an empty cafe secured with a heavy-duty lock (our contact with the outside world was facilitated by a small window).

Where was I to go without pants? Who could I tell?

Esenin showed up half an hour later. Having seen my distressed face in the window and heard my tale of woe, he collapsed on the sidewalk laughing and coughing till the tears ran down his face.

Then he brought me his gray lounge suit. Esenin came up to my shoulders, while his pants came down to my shins. I looked quite the fop in them indeed!

While we were riding the suburban Moscow train, a small piece of burning coal from the engine flew in through the window and burned a hole the size of a 20-kopeck piece in the trousers Esenin had lent me.

Esenin stopped laughing and, moving me to a seat away from the window, covered the jacket he'd lent me with a newspaper. Then he started cursing the Allies because of whom engines had to be stoked with God knows what; me, for sleeping like a log (you could carry the log away without it hearing a thing); and the friend who had persuaded us — idiots — to drag ourselves out to his dacha.

Meanwhile, a pink patch of skin gazed out from the hole, six inches above my knee.

'It's a good thing you didn't bring me some drawers, Sergei,' I said, 'or they would've been burned too.'

10

I was sitting in the Poets' Cafe scrutinizing the nose of critic Vyacheslav Polonsky, then on-stage, recalling a pink signal flag on a holiday garland.

What an amazing nose! There was nothing like it in all Moscow!

A cartoon by the artist Mak showed the corner of a building and a nose sticking out from behind: 'Five minutes before the appearance of Polonsky.'

'Indeed, even Meyerhold's nose is a good inch shorter,' I thought. 'How disproportionally nature lavishes her gifts!'

A jab in my ribs awoke me from my reverie.

Squinting his eyes somewhere toward the floor, Esenin said:

'Moses, may I present my best friend, Tolya.'

Then just audibly in my ear:

'A patron.'

I had read about patrons of the arts in French novels and in collections of old-fashioned anecdotes about the lives and whims of various Russian oddballs. I'd heard from one decrepit fellow about Ryabushinsky's 'Black Swan' and *The Golden Fleece*, a journal he had published in several languages, with gilded letters and insert sheets of the most delicate rice paper — which for the *The Golden Fleece* was really too much, since its only readers were none other than the poets themselves, deemed worthy of the golden letter treatment.

But a pa-a-atron in the fle-e-esh, and what's more in the days of War Communism, and in Red Moscow, and for good measure one who in the third minute of

Nikolai Ryabushinsky, Russian magnate and patron of the arts, belonged to the Ryabushinsky family of big bankers and merchants. In the 1910s his villa 'Black Swan' in Moscow was famous for its sumptuous parties for the 'gilded youth'.

our acquaintance had already twisted off a button from my vest — oh my! Never had I thought, in my sleeping or w-w-waking dreams, of meeting such a patron.

He was ruddy, pudgy, and roly-poly, like a young spud fried in butter, with a chick's fine down on his head. His family once owned some factories near Moscow, Saratov, and Nizhny Novgorod, and in all these cities they used to have houses, homes and hovels. He was so short that if I had stood on tiptoe and he had bent a little at the knees, he could have passed under my legs, as under the Triumphal Arch. Later on, so as not to provoke people's laughter, we never walked next to each other on the street; we always put Esenin in the middle.

Even more remarkable was his manner of speech: he pronounced hushings like whistlings, whistlings like hushings, gutturals like nasals, nasals like gutturals; he made the short vowels long, the long vowels short, and as for accents — well, here there were no limits to his inventiveness and fantasy.

Despite all this he worshiped the Latin classics, modern poetry and Derzhavin for his *Felitsa*.

Gavrila Derzhavin (1743-1816), leading poet of his time, founder of Russian Classicism.

Seated on the spine of an armchair (I never saw him sit in a place actually designed for sitting), he loved to say:

'Khings weren't sso ssilly, when they ssurrounded themselvess with poetss ... Sserge, read "The Little Birrch..."'

Tired of knocking about without a home, Esenin and I moved into his flat.

After the rooms at the Europa Hotel, the inquisitorial couch at the Writers' Union, nights spent at friends' places on beds made of two chairs that split apart under you right when sleep was at its sweetest, and nights staying with girlfriends to whom our hearts were cold, the soft hair mattresses of our patron, the fine cotton linen and downy blankets, all reconciled us to the many disadvantages deriving from his tender friendship.

Besides his love for poetry, he also suffered from an overstimation of his commercial talents, seriously believing himself to be an incomparable schemer and wheeler-dealer of the latest stamp.

Esenin — a virtuoso at playing on weak human strings — set himself the unswerving task of extracting money from him for an Imagist press.

The inducements began — long, persistent, seductive. Esenin painted pictures of glory for him like that of Sytin, of a place in the history of literature like that of Smirdin and ... of a three hundred percent return on his investment.

As a result — at the end of the second week of inducements — we received twelve thousand in Kerensky notes.

On that memorable day an old man in gold-rimmed spectacles was dining over at our capitalist's. Not so long before he had been 'the richest Jew in Russia.' But now he neither schemed, nor sold his houses (requisitioned by the Soviet authorities), nor invested in any 'sure things' with a three hundred percent return.

Our patron, condescendingly patting the old man on the knee, said:

'You should retire, Israel Israelevich! What's to do, indeed, now that there are no more commercial ideas.'

Ivan Sytin (1851-1934) the biggest publisher in Russia in the beginning of the 20th century. Known for his series of cheap editions of Russian classics, popular science books, encyclopedias and calendars.

Alexander Smirdin (1795-1857) publisher and bookseller. Published first editions of Pushkin, Gogol, and other Russian authors. He was the first in Russia to introduce author's remuneration.

Kerensky notes, see next page.

Kerensky notes, or *Kerenki*, named after Kerensky, Prime Minister of the Provisional Government. In the post-revolutionary years both old and new currencies were used, including the money issued by various provisional governments.

And then he recounted how he himself — a man of the latest stamp — had just completed a deal with such commercially hopeless material as two poets:

'Why not make twenty-four thousand from twelve. Like the Russian proverb says, "It won't hurt the birdie to peck here and there." '

The intelligent old Jew's gold-rimmed spectacles gleamed; he smoothed his gray beard and smiled softly.

Some three months later the first small book from our press appeared.

By that time Esenin and I were renting a room in Bakhrushin's house on Bogoslovsky Lane.

'The patron' appeared unexpectedly on our doorstep.

Esenin greeted him with outstretched arms and presented him with a copy of the book, quite fresh and smelling sweetly of printer's ink, with a touching inscription.

The man thanked him, kissed him and asked for his thirty-six thousand.

Esenin promised to personally bring it round to his flat in a few days.

Three short weeks later, a little collection of our verse came out.

And once again our patron was at the door.

We immediately handed him the second book, with an even more touching inscription.

This time he agreed to remit twelve thousand and to earn for himself a return of a mere one hundred percent or so on the deal.

Esenin pressed his hand and thanked him for his good will and magnanimity.

The third meeting took place just before Christmas. He came upon us in the street. We were walking in a huff, practically purple with rage; it was the third day we'd been eating flour dissolved in cold water, slightly sugared. The paste coated the gullet, lay like a lump in the stomach, and did nothing to relieve hunger.

Doggedly buttonholing us both, he said:

'I've decided, boys, that I don't need your return. You take your twenty-four, and I'll take my twelve ... How about it? Shall we shake on it?'

And we shook hands, our cold palms against his warm one.

The last meeting I don't even want to remember...

It was a warm March day. We were bouncing along in a draught cart, our legs dangling, conveying five thousand copies of our brand-new book from the press to Tsentropechat.

Suddenly he turned up.

The conversation was short. Esenin climbed down reluctantly from the stacks of books. I followed. The cart turned a corner, and instead of Tsentropechat, set off for Kamergersky Lane — to go and heat our patron's magnificent marble bathroom, with our verse as fuel.

My right nostril tickled unpleasantly. I tried to convince myself that I really wanted to sneeze — it would have been faint-hearted to think anything else. In parting, the portly man with chick's down for hair reminded me:

'For pity's sake, Anatoly. I knew your mother and father. They were very, very honest people.'

I glanced at Esenin. When the cart with our books

had passed out of view, a tear — large and heavy, like the first drop of rain — fell from his eyelashes.

Yesterday I was leafing through Chekhov. In his spellbinding story 'Gooseberries' a merchant on his deathbed orders a plate of molasses brought to him. He eats all his money and bonds with the molasses, so that no one will get them after he's gone.

11

Four stallions rear up over the Bolshoi Theater. They rip the reins, strain their leg muscles. And it's all to no avail, the huge columned building stays put.

Esenin looked up:

'You and I are like those stupid horses. Russian literature seems to be heavier than the Bolshoi Theater.'

For the third time he started rereading a little article in a journal.

The article savaged Esenin. It was signed: *Oleg Leonidov.*

I took the journal from Esenin's hands, twisted it into a tube and put it in my pocket.

'Once they wrote that Pushkin and Baratynsky were pimples on the skin of widowed Russian literature.'

Esenin would catch every word — disparaging or flattering — spoken about his verse and store it in his memory. He could rush from one end of Moscow to the other for the sake of ten lines printed about him in some insignificant little gazette. Those who wrote or spoke ill of him as a poet were his mortal enemies.

In 1918, a certain Georgy Gayer demolished Esenin in a Futurist journal.

Gayer's main point was that: 'Esenin's urbanity clashes with his peasant origin.'

Futurist positions in those days took no prisoners.

Two years later, Esenin inadvertently discovered that 'Georgy Gayer' was actually Vadim Shershenevich.

He grew cold towards Shershenevich, like ice. I expended copious amounts of verbal warmth to melt this iceberg a bit from the top.

Still, Esenin never fully forgave Shershenevich that little article.

'Georgy Gayer,' he would snarl.

12

We were standing near the Metropol and eating apples. The artist Deed Ladeau passed by in a cab loaded with luggage.

'Where you off to, Deed?'

'Petersburg.'

We ran across the square to him as fast as our legs would carry us.

'Just how are you getting there?'

'In a first-class carriage, in a private compartment of red velvet.'

'With whom?'

'With a Red Commissar. A most hideous one! Decked with pistols and daggers, like a Christmas tree with crackers. And his noggin's like a shaven beet.'

According to his passport Deed was past fifty, but in spirit he was eighteen. The English have a wonderful saying: 'A suit's only as old as it looks.'

Deed had painted the walls of Strastnoi Monastery

In 1919 Imagists covered the walls of the Strastnoi Monastery in Moscow with their theomachist verse and pictures. They also put up street signs re-naming some streets after their own heroes. For example, Tverskaya Street was re-named Esenin Street. The street sign remained on display for a month.

with us, he had changed the names on street signs, he'd hung a placard, 'I'm with the Imagists', on the cast-iron Pushkin.

At the Writer's Union he delivered a lecture on 'snoutography', showing with the help of his pencil drawings the likeness of all the Imagists to horses: Esenin was a Vyatka, Shershenevich an Orlov, and I a Hunter.

Deed had a sharp eye.

We even took to calling Esenin 'Vyatka' among ourselves.

'Deed, take us with you.'

'Just like that, without hats?'

'What the hell do we need them for?'

If one is 'eighteen,' what does he care?

'Have you got any money?'

'It's not America we're going to.'

'Come on, jump in.'

We set off for Nikolaevsky Station.

Nikolayevsky Station is now called Leningradsky Station.

The commissar was standing on the platform, next to his private carriage.

His eyes were round and cold, like silver rubles. His head too was round, without a single hair, and bright red.

I whispered into Deed's ear:

'Ach, "the beet" won't take us!'

But Esenin was already fingering his pistol and discussing the advantages of a Colt over a revolver, exalting the steel of the Caucasian saber and the mellow chime of the spur.

A film director once made a movie about Jewish life. In the last part, during a pogrom scene, a two-year-old tot was supposed to cry bitter tears in close-up. The director found a charming little boy with golden curls. The shoot began. The floodlights flashed on. Practically all children — afraid of bright light, humming, the black eye of the camera and strange 'uncles' — burst into bitter tears. But this one wasn't the least perturbed, grinning from ear to ear. They tried this and that — the kid just wouldn't give in. The director threw up his hands. Then the mother of the 'undejected' child told the director:

'You tell him, comrade, "Moisha, take off your shoes!" He hates to and always cries.'

The director spoke the words and — the studio resounded with a piercing shriek. The bitter tears flowed in a stream. The cameraman cranked his camera.

Esenin, like that mother, knew exactly everybody's secret, their 'Moisha's shoes,' he knew how to make people like him, to turn hearts, to win souls.

Hence his enormous charm.

Usually, we love those who love us. Esenin loved no one, and everybody loved Esenin.

Of course the commissar took us with him in his railway carriage, of course we set off for Petersburg and slept on red velvet and drank his Caucasian wines.

In Petersburg the whole first day we ran around to publishing houses. At World Literature Publishing House Esenin introduced me to Blok. I liked Blok for his conventionality. He would have fit right in in some Soviet ministry, presiding over blue office documents, the little unexpected joys of the day, the incoming and outgoing directives.

Blok, see p.21

The second day in Petersburg it rained.

The part in my hair gleamed like the lid of a grand piano. Esenin's golden head turned brown, and his curls drooped like the pitiful commas of a clerk. He was absolutely miserable about it.

In the years of War Communism, due to severe shortages, all consumer goods were rationed, they were sold only on presenting ration coupons, issued at one's place of work.

We ran from shop to shop, pleading with them to sell us a hat without a coupon.

In one store, a red-cheeked German behind the till said finally:

'Without a coupon I can only let you have top hats.'

Overjoyed beyond words, we gratefully pressed the German's pudgy hand.

Five minutes later on Nevsky Prospect the ghostly Petersburgers were goggling at us, the candy vendors laughed at us, and a startled policeman demanded our papers.

That is the true story of the first appearance of the legendary top hats (quite singular for the revolution), glorified in rumor and hymned by poets.

13

By the fall we were living in the Bakhrushin house. Karp Karpovich Korotkov — a poet little known to readers, but quite popular in literary circles — let us stay at his apartment.

Karp Karpovich was the son of a rich manufacturer, but even before the Revolution he had left his family home and devoted himself to the arts.

Soon he had released some thirty books, all distinguished for their unprecedented lack of sales and their Eastern accents on Russian words.

Nonetheless the books disappeared pretty quickly

thanks to the inexpressible energy with which Karp Karpovich himself handed them out, along with his autograph!

One joker even promised two pounds of Ukrainian lard to any eccentric who might have a copy of Karp Karpovich's books without a dedicatory inscription.

This was no small gamble. In 1919, not only for the sake of lard, but even for yellow millet, people would feed lice with their bodies for weeks in the icy carriages.

All the same our joker had to eat his own lard himself.

Our room was big and quite nice.

14

There is no force capable of separating a Russian from his ruinous devotion to the arts — not a typhoid louse; nor ankle-deep provincial mud; nor 'loo-lessness'; nor war; nor revolution; nor an empty stomach.

You might say we have refined natures.

I was returning home late one night from a friend's. In the sky hung a cloud like a rustic washstand with a broken faucet — a cursed rain flowed freely and without respite.

The Tverskaya pavement was black and glossy — just like my top hat.

I was meaning to turn onto Kozitsky Lane. Suddenly from the opposite side of the street I hear:

'Hey, foreigner, stop!'

I tended to fluster simpletons; my top hat and wide overcoat, you see.

Five men moved away from a wall.

I waited.

'Citizen foreigner, your identity card!'

Nearby, a cabman driving a jade roan hobbled along the dilapidated roadway. He glanced in our direction — then whipped his Bucephalus. The latter, being no fool, gallopped off. A guard was dozing off by the Cafe Lyre. Before my eyes, he darted into a by-street and — cheers!

Not a living soul. Not even a stray dog. Or a dim street lamp.

I asked them:

'By what right, comrades, do you demand documents of me? Your warrant?'

'Warrant ...?'

A fellow in a student's peak-cap, with a face that was pale and rumpled — like a pillow after a night's sleep — waved a pistol in my face:

'Here's your warrant, comrade, right here!'

'So, perhaps this isn't about my papers. But my overcoat!'

'Well, hurrah for you, God bless ... You guessed it.'

The fellow with the rumpled face stood behind me, gently helping me disrobe, like the doorman at a good hotel.

I tried to joke. But it wasn't a very happy occasion.

I'd just had the overcoat made. A good cut, high quality thick woolen cloth.

Rumple-face stared at me sadly.

But just as I was slipping out of my sleeves in complete despair, that selfsame Russian love for art, a love that knows no bounds, came to my rescue.

One of the group, staring at me intently, asked:

'And what, comrade, might your name be?'

'Mariengof...'

'Anatoly Mariengof?'

Pleasantly stunned at the extent of my fame, I repeated with pride:

'Anatoly Mariengof!'

'The author of *Magdalene*?'

At this happy and magical moment of my life I would have given them not only my overcoat, but thrown in my pants, patent-leather boots, silk socks, and handkerchief as well.

Let it rain! Let me go back home in just my underpants! Let our budget be shot to hell! Let it, a thousand times let it!

What a succulent and rich food for my ambition, that voracious Falstaff we carry in our hearts!

Needless to say, my nocturnal acquaintances didn't touch the overcoat; the ringleader, having discovered in my person the Mariengof, was profuse in his apologies; they escorted me all the way home and in parting I warmly shook their hands and invited them to come hear my new stuff at Pegasus' Stall.

Pegasus' Stall, a poets' cafe that existed until 1924 when it went bankrupt.

Two days later there was more confirmation of the Russians' refined nature.

Esenin dropped in on the cobbler. He needed his soles patched.

The cobbler quoted a fair price. Esenin, without haggling, left him an address for delivery:

'Bogoslovsky 3, apartment 46 — Esenin.'

The cobbler clasped his hands:

'Esenin!'

And in a fit of rapture he cut the price in half.

A page of history (true, the circumstances were somewhat different, but also noteworthy):

Gatchina, a royal residence outside St Petersburg, military headquarters during WWI.

The year is 1917. In Gatchina General Krasnov, commanding Kerensky's forces, concludes an inglorious accord with the Bolshevik detachments.

In comes Kerensky's adjutant and Lev Trotsky. They are followed by a Cossack guard with a rifle. The Cossack catches hold of Trotsky's sleeve and won't let go.

Trotsky turns to Krasnov:

'General, order your Cossack to leave us alone.'

Pyotr Krasnov (1869-1947) led the anti-Soviet uprising in 1917 and commanded the White Cossacks Army in 1918. In 1919, emigrated to Germany where he indeed wrote a novel and memoirs. Executed by the Soviets for his collaboration with the Nazi.

Krasnov pretends not to recognize Trotsky.

'And just who are you?'

'I am Trotsky.'

The Cossack stands at attention before Krasnov:

'Yer excellency, I was stationed to guard the Mister Officer here (Kerensky's adjutant), and alluva sudden this here little Jewboy comes in and says, "I am Trotsky, come with me." I'm a guard. So I follows 'em. I ain't lettin' go without the corporal 'a the guard here.'

'Ach, how stupid!' Trotsky spits out and leaves, slamming the door.

General Krasnov then turns to his officers with a phrase worthy of immortality.

'What a magnificent scene for my future novel!'

Russians, Russians!

Here we have the irreversible setting of the general's sun. The surrender of Petersburg. Russia's fate is at stake. And he, commander of the army (true, only two companies and nine hundred Cossacks, but still decisive:

to be or not to be), expounds upon a scene for a novel? How do you like that?

15

In those days a man was stronger than a horse.

Horses would fall on the streets, die and clutter the roadways with their carcasses. A man would find the strength to drag himself as far as a stable and, if there was nothing else for it but to stretch out his legs, he'd do that behind a stone wall and under an iron roof.

Esenin and I were walking along Myasnitskaya Street.

The number of horse carcasses, tallied up by our shocked eyes, exceeded by an order of three the number of blocks from our own Bogoslovsky Lane to the Garden Ring Road.

Opposite the Main Post Office lay two bloated carcasses, one black, missing a tail, the other white with bared teeth.

Atop the white one sat two ravens, pecking eye-jelly out of the hollow sockets. A snub-nosed candy vendor in a brown bowler hat on his tow-haired little head, tossed a rock at them. The ravens waved their black wings and cawed back some abuse of their own.

A dog was gnawing on the second cadaver. A cabman passing by on a mud-splattered sleigh flogged it with his whip. The dog pulled its snout, long and narrow like a sharpened pencil, out of the cavity where the horse's tail had once been. The dog's eyes showed annoyance, its white snout covered to the ears in blood, as if wearing a red mask. The cur licked its chops with relish.

The whole way back we walked in silence. It was snowing.

Entering our room, we threw our coats onto the chairs, not bothering to shake the flakes off them. It was below zero in the room. The snow on the coats didn't melt.

A red-haired girl brought us a small electric heater. The girl loved poetry — and one of us, to boot.

We never did manage to find out which one, due to our tireless pursuit of glory and the endless obstacles then. Reminiscing about this later on, we both regretted it — the girl had big blue eyes and hair the color of maple leaves in September.

The heater brought us no small comfort.

When we sat down to write verse, we would lock the door, turning the key twice in the lock, and with a criminal air we'd set the heater up on the table. That our ink didn't freeze in the inkwell and that we could write without gloves on was cause for celebration.

Electric heaters were strictly forbidden; we were committing a crime against the Revolution.

Around two in the morning Arseny Avraamov would come for the heater. He was finishing his book, *The Incarnation* (about us), and in his room at the Nerenzee house the ink would also freeze and the snow on his galoshes wouldn't melt. What's more, Arseny had no gloves. He said that without the heater his fingers became like icicles — if he tried to bend them, they'd snap off.

The 10-story Nerenzee house, built by the architect Nerenzee in 1912, was the tallest building in Moscow at that time.

I note all this down so you'll read Esenin's *Mare Ships* more attentively: a remarkable poem about 'the ripped-open stomachs of mares, with their black sails of ravens'; about 'the sun, cooling like a puddle made by a gelding'; about 'hard frost skipping along the fields'; and about 'dogs sucking the edge of dawn with famished mouths.'

Since then a lot of water has flowed under the bridge. The Bakhrushin house now has central heating; at Nerenzee's there are gas stoves and bathrooms that warm up in a few minutes, while Esenin rose to fame at last, the day after his death.

16

Having endured many a dull hour in the reception room of the Moscow City Council, we finally received a permit from Kamenev to open a bookshop.

There were already two writers' bookshops in existence. Mikhail Osorgin, Boris Zaitsev, the poet Vladislav Khodasevich, professor Nikolai Berdyaev and some others from the old 'union of writers' ran a shop in Leontyevsky Lane.

It was a respectable firm, its owners with well-groomed heads of hair and their place in the annals of Russian belles-lettres assured.

Provincial intellectuals with Chekhovian beards would walk out of the shop moved to tears — like old women leaving the presence of the wonderworking Iverskaya Icon.

In Kamergersky Lane, Shershenevich and Kusikov stood behind the counter of the other bookshop.

Shershenevich did everything very professionally: verse, theater, feuilletons; he played tennis and poker

Mikhail Osorgin (1878-1942), writer. Evicted from Russia in 1922.

Boris Zaitsev (1881-1972), writer, chairman of the Moscow Writers Union in 1921-22. Emigrated to Paris in 1922.

Vladislav Khodasevich (1886-1939), poet. Emigrated in 1922 with his wife Nina Berberova.

Nikolai Berdyaev (1874-1948) was appointed professor of philosophy at Moscow University after the 1917 Revolution but evicted in 1922 because of his religious views. He settled in France.

professionally; he fell in love, made witticisms, ran an office professionally — and spoke (ooooh, how he spoke).

He ran his business professionally, too. He would divide the visitors to his store into 'purchasers' and 'putterers.'

The manager of the cafe at Pegasus' Stall, Anatoly Silin, without the slightest irony, had his own classification of the visitors: 'serious' and 'not serious.' He relegated all composers, painters and actors ('the idle', in the parlance of the rabble) to the 'not serious' camp. While traders from flea markets such as Sukharevka, Okhotny Ryad and Smolensky — die-hard embezzlers and unmuzzled thieves, along with their mirthful wenches — he lumped in the 'serious' category.

Having received the permit for our shop, Esenin and I began to scour the city in search of a place and partners.

At that time we had not a penny in our pockets. To open the shop we needed — besides the space — such trifles as money and books.

It took us some effort to get a space on Nikitskaya Street, in the building of the Conservatory.

We had a writ. A little old man from the Conservatory had the key.

They warned us at the Ministry:

Anatoly Lunacharsky (1875-1933) the Commissar for Education from 1917 to 1929.

'Get ahold of the keys and the shop's yours. If you don't get them, we're not going to court to get them for you. And mind you, the old man is a mean one, he has some kind of mandate from Lunacharsky.'

We lay in wait for the mean old fogie at the entrance

to the shop. On the fourth day, shaking his disheveled gray mane, he stuck the key in the lock.

Esenin jabbed me in the side:

'Start talking to grandpa.'

'T-t-t-talking...?' And my eyes rolled up to my forehead. 'I'm afraid of mopheads! And what am I gonna talk to him about?'

'How about a dog's hernia, you blockhead!'

The second jab in my side was more persuasive than the first and I reluctantly pulled off my hat before the gray mane that had just knocked the gift of speech and thought out of me.

'Pardon me, would you do me a favor... Well, you see... You would oblige me greatly, if... if, uh, you would deign to say a word or two about Schubert, or, uh, let's say, Chopin...'

'What?!'

'Please be good enough to understand, I've been interested in counterpoint for the longest time and...'

Esenin approvingly and imperiously nodded his head.

'... and B-flats,' he intervened.

With the key left sticking out of the lock, the mane sympathetically offered me his hand.

'I've got it.' Esenin muttered.

The mean old fogie started to howl and grabbed Esenin by the flap of his coat — in the pocket of which the long-dreamt-of key lightly clinked.

Esenin ruthlessly disengaged the other's hand from his flap and, pulling the writ with the violet seal out of his wallet, he stuck it under the old man's nose.

On this hard-hearted day, you might say, we launched the fragile little ship of our prosperity.

As for financial partners, there was no shortage of them.

17

Right in the middle of the bustle surrounding the launch of our 'fragile little ship,' some guests turned up out of the blue at our place on Bogoslovsky.

Zinaida Raikh (1894-1939) Esenin's first wife (1917-18) by whom he had two children. In 1922 she married the famous stage director Vsevolod Meyerhold (1874-1940) who made a star out of her. She was murdered by secret service agents shortly before the execution of Meyerhold.

Esenin's wife, Zinaida Nikolayevna Raikh arrived from Oryol. She brought with her their little daughter — she had to be shown to her father. Tanya wasn't yet a year old.

The other guest was our bosom buddy from Penza, Mikhail Molabukh.

Zinaida Nikolayevna, little Tanya, her nanny, Molabukh and the two of us — six souls inside four walls!

What's more, little Tanya — as they used to write in ancient children's books — was 'brightly, sprightly, won't-leave a-live-stool-without-a-fightly'. She went from the nanny's lap to Zinaida Nikolayevna's, from her to Molabukh, from him to me. It was only her father's 'live stool' that she couldn't stand at all. We even tried trickery and flattery and bribery and severity — all to no avail.

Esenin became frankly angry: he didn't take at all kindly to what he considered 'Raikh's machinations.'

Zinaida Nikolayevna had a lump in her throat at the shame for Tanya not warming to her father.

As usual humor went side by side with grief. The

second word out of Molabukh's mouth (just as all sorts of meat and pies were being unpacked) was:

'Do you know how much fer salt in Penza?'

'How much?'

'Seven thousand.'

'Not really!'

'Upon my word.'

We went to lunch at about two. In Gazetny Lane at Nadezhda Adelheim's small antique shop. In the front room stood a three-legged table, a mahogany wardrobe and a dusty glass case. Under the turbid glass, on frayed velvet: a small snuff box, two or three cameos and 17th-century china cups (one cracked, one without a handle, another minus its saucer).

In the back room the charming Nadezhda Adelheim served us meals.

Molabukh asked, over coffee:

'Do you know, boys, how much fer salt in Penza?'

'How much?'

'Nine thousand.'

'Oho!'

'Here's your oho.'

In the evening Tanya's nanny set up the samovar for us. She used boards from the fence for fuel. Today I can confess it: in our building's courtyard some very healthy poplars were enclosed by a fence, for no reason at all. Esenin and I, lying in bed one night curled up in a ball against the cold, decided:

'What's the use of having fences around poplars for nothing! This is no time for things like that.'

We started fueling our samovar with the fence. If

our neighbors hadn't followed our example that fence would have lasted us the rest of the Revolution.

On the evening in question we feasted on Penza veal, Moscow pastries, Oryol sugar and white bread.

Salting his veal, Molabukh asked ponderously:

'And how much, you figure, fer salt in Penza?'

'Well, how much?'

'Eleven thousand.'

Esenin looked at him with laughing eyes and, as if nothing were amiss, let drop:

'Mm-hmm ... so just today it's gone up by four thousand rubles...'

And we roared with uncontrollable laughter.

Molabukh's cheekbones trembled:

'How's that?'

'Very simple: this morning it was seven, over coffee it was nine, and now it's leapt up to eleven.'

We roared again.

From then on we called Molabukh 'How-Much-fer-Salt.'

He was a marvelous fellow, only he was terribly absent-minded and had a short memory. Every time he mentioned a car he'd had at his disposal on the German front, it had a different make and its driver a different name. At dinner he would mistakenly pour water from a carafe into his glass instead of vodka. After downing the glass as if it were vodka, he'd wheeze and, smacking his lips, have a bite of herring.

You'd say to him:

'What are you wheezing for?'

'Hm?'

'I said, what are you wheezing for?'

'It's stro-o-ong!'

'It's stro-o-ong, all right... Boiled, probably... It's water.'

Then he'd turn livid; he'd spit in disgust and finally drown his vexation in vodka to the point of stupor.

Once on a train from Sevastopol to Simferopol, instead of wine, he drained an entire glass of red ink in one gulp. He smelled it only on the last gulp. He was so terrified that he changed into some clean underwear and a shirt and lay on his bunk preparing to surrender his soul to God.

He didn't surrender his soul, though he did have terrible stomach ache.

18

Tenderly putting his arm around my shoulder and fixing his blue eyes on my pupils, Esenin asked:

'Do you love me, Anatoly? Are you a true friend of mine or not?'

'What're you babbling about?'

'Just this ... I can't live with Zinaida ... I swear to you I can't ... I told her — she won't understand ... She's not leaving and that's that ... She won't leave, not for anything ... She's gotten it into her head, "You love me, Sergei, I know it and don't tell me you don't." You tell her, Tolya (I can't beg any harder than I'm begging you now!) — tell her there's another woman.'

'Are you mad, Sergei?'

'Are you a friend or not? To me, her love is a noose... Tolya, sweet Tolya, I'll go for a walk... on the boulevard, near the river... and you tell her — she'll ask for sure — tell her that I'm at the other woman's... that I've been seeing her since spring, and I'm crazy about her. Let me kiss you.'

The next day Zinaida Nikolayevna went back to Oryol.

19

In the 1880s, Princess Zinaida Volkonskaya held a literary evening for the Russian colony in Rome. Gogol read *The Inspector General* in manuscript. There was a large crowd at first. But after the first act, to Volkonskaya's horror, half the audience left. Gogol read the second act and the crowd grew even thinner. The same thing happened after the third act, too. The memoirist concludes, 'It was only thanks to the princess' enchanting powers of persuasion that she managed to retain a small circle of her closest friends around the cheerless lector.'

Man's stupidity is boundless.

Two students came to our bookshop: dog-fur caps, blue collars showing from under their coats. I caught sight of their noses — law students for sure. And so it was: a certain familiarity in their manners, the most repulsive ease in their words.

'We would like to see the poets Esenin and Mariengof.'

Since childhood I've had an irrational dislike of student's peak-caps; 'Gaudeamus' threw me into frenzy. Judging the students in the upper classes at school more obtuse even than army staff-captains, I dreamed of going to a university abroad.

And wasn't it the perfect course of fate for the Russian student body, in the war years, to fill up the military academies, and become *bona fide* cadets and ensigns? In the days of Kerensky, on the fields of Galicia, they exposed their own necks to German bullets to rouse the spirits of their reluctant soldiers. (I like the joke about the Jew who makes it to the front line and the first thing he says is, 'Say, where can I give myself up here?')

In October 1917, down to the last cartridge and the last machine-gun belt they returned fire from behind the walls of their military colleges. And in the decisive hour they went off on the 'Icy Campaign' to replace Kornilov's Cossacks, whom the general had to urge: 'Shoot me first, then give yourselves up to the Bolsheviks. I would rather be shot by you.' He did not have to persuade the students long.

The blue collars were rummaging through Imagist publications, while Esenin and I whispered in a corner.

'At their place? ... A club? ... Perform? ... To hell with them, I won't go.'

'Drop it, Anatoly, we're going ... It's awkward ... But then, anyway it'll be fun — they're students.'

On the first floor of a building in Bronnaya Street, a long, narrow hall with yellow windows and a low ceiling. Body to body, like books on a shelf, when you're thinking whether you can squeeze one more in. Lots and lots of blue collars! And darned if the elbows on their uniform jackets hadn't worn thin, even in the third year of the Revolution.

Esenin came out onto the stage. He smiled, narrowed his lids and, as he always did, put out one

Lavr Kornilov (1870-1918) army general. In August 1917 led the uprising against the Soviets and organized the White Army.

'Icy Campaign' — in January 1918, as the White Army, led by General Kornilov, was retreating to the South it came across a frozen river. Kornilov was killed in action while General Markov commanded his regiment to cross the river and himself stepped into the icy water followed by his men. Later Kornilov's campaign was called after this episode.

spellbinding hand. The hand lived as one with his verse, the way a rhythmic pendulum lives as one with a clock.

He began:

Light rain cleanses with wet brooms...

Someone sniggered in the back of the hall.

Willow branch droppings in the valleys...

There was wall-to-wall chuckling and some sniggers in the back.

Spit, you wind, leaves by the armful...

Chuckles sprinkled down like silver five-kopeck pieces in the front rows, and fell like heavy ruble coins in the back ones.

Somebody whistled.

I love to see the dark blue thickets,
Like heavy-footed oxen,
The wheezing stomachs of their foliage
Staining the knees...

He didn't manage to get out the words, '*of tree trunks.*' The entire hall chock-full of blue collars and golden buttons was howling, wailing, whistling and stamping its feet.

Esenin smiled childishly. At a loss, he drank in this scene with wide-open eyes. He stood there in silence for several seconds and then shuffled off the stage.

For the first time, I saw Esenin disoriented onstage. He clearly was astonished at this reception.

We had had our baptism of fire. In answer to the Politechnical hall's whine, he stuck two fingers in his mouth and gave such a piercing whistle that the raging, thousand-headed howl abruptly stopped.

Esenin turned his ashen face to me:

'Tolya, what is this?'

'It's nothing, Sergei. Just students.'

When we came out onto Bronnaya, a girl ran up to us. Tears streaming down her puffy little cheeks and her rosy, hitched-up, round little nose just below her brows.

'I was there ... I ... I ... saw ... Comrade Esenin ... Comrade Mariengof ... You ... You ... You ...'

The girl must've thought that right from Bronnaya we were off to the Moscow River to find ourselves a suitable ice hole.

Esenin took her hands:

'Good, splendiferous young lady, we're going to a cafe ... Do you hear, a cafe ... 18 Tverskaya, to drink coffee and have some cakes.'

'Really?'

'Really.'

'Promise?'

'Promise.'

I caught sight of this girl at Esenin's funeral. Locking eyes with her, I recalled our touching acquaintance and recounted it to a cold, unfamiliar hall.

Have you any idea, oh splendiferous young lady, that Esenin affectionately nicknamed you 'Collarpuss,' that we loved you and remembered you for the rest of our years?

20

'The boy's wasting away ... I can't look — it makes you want to c-c-cry. I love 'im after all, the stinker. Y'understand, I love 'im with all my guts.'

'Who's wasting away, Sergei? Who're you talking about?'

'About Molabukh, I'm telling you. Our poor How-Much-fer-Salt is wasting away. Makes you wanna c-c-cry...'

Esenin started to expound upon our friend's ruin. And indeed, his life was running its course without any purpose. Neither his worries nor his joys were his own.

'He's conked out 'til twelve, the rat bastard. He loafs around while we're grinding away at our poems. He chases after us without a scent, like some hound after a fox: to the printer's, to the shop, after someone else's glory. Even at the Strastnoi Monastery he painted his name right next to ours: Mikhail Molabukh.'

He was referring to the theomachist verse that we scrolled on the thick monastery walls.

Esenin sighed dejectedly:

'And not for anything — the sod — does he want to work. He doesn't know what's good for him. I asked him yesterday: "Come on, How-Much-fer-Salt, you used to ride around in your separate train carriage on soft springs — that means maybe Soviet Russia could use you?" And he says: "I dunno ..." I tell you, it makes you wanna cry-y-y.'

So as to save How-Much-fer-Salt, Esenin proposed we evict him from our common household.

Our punishment was cruel.

More than anything else in life How-Much-fer-Salt loved good company and good food. In all of Moscow, you could find both only at the round table of Nadezhda Adelheim.

Once Esenin and I, stubby pencils in hand, added up the modest price of our dinner, and it depressed us no end: it turned out that at one sitting, we had each consumed 250 copies of a 48-page booklet of verse. Even for a grown elephant, this would've been no small amount.

The portion allotted for How-Much-fer-Salt's dinner came out to a hundred copies. Nadezhda Adelheim's pleasant company was now for him irretrievably lost.

At five, setting out for dinner, we all went together as far as the corner of Gazetny Lane. There we parted ways. Every time our goodbyes were tragic. Our friend's cheekbones bounced like bony balls. Peering in despair at Esenin's galoshes, he pleaded in barely audible tones:

'Just fer once more, Seryozha! I wanna go with you so badly ... have Adelheim's pork cutlet fer the la-a-ast time.'

'No!'

'No?'

'No!'

Taking their lead from the yellow balls of How-Much-fer-Salt's cheekbones, his upper lip (a red ball) and his pupils (black balls) started bouncing too.

Poor How-Much-fer-Salt!

During the retreat from Riga with his 'Bathhouse Detachment' he slept one night on the wet ground under his cart's awning. From then on those little balls in his face kept bouncing, the names of drivers and the makes of cars kept getting mixed up in his head and his bones ached in bad weather and thaws.

Dear How-Much-fer-Salt, let's you and I together hate the war and admire that character from the anecdote. You know who I'm talking about. After all, you and I together gasped with laughter over him.

A certain chemist prepared pills in a pharmacy and sold enemas. Then the war came. They sent him to the front line and plopped him down in a trench. He sits there, with nothing for his pains. Boom! An explosion. Boom! Another. Boom! A third. The trench fills with meat, rocks, bones, rags, blood and lead. The chemist jumps out and, waving his arms, bawls out to the Germans: 'You maniacs, what are you doing? There are people sitting in here!'

But you're in no mood for jokes, my dear How-Much-fer-Salt. You feel like crying, not laughing.

We, 'the swine,' are on our way to eat cutlets while we grudge you ('Some friends you are!') dinner, sending you ('You'll eat us dry!') to swallow any old carrion ('Your own stomachs have probably smarted from this dreck!') in that basement dive.

How-Much-fer-Salt is talking almost inaudibly — with only his lips, his eyes, his heart:

'Seryozha, please, just fer one last time...'

Esenin spread his hands apart:

'Nn-no.'

How-Much-fer-Salt's back, green in its winter overcoat, would dive for the gate and quickly, posthaste, run off to the basement where a red-haired cook with a halo created his phantasmagoria.

Meanwhile, we turned the corner.

'Let him go... Just let him... (And Esenin scratched the small of his neck) The boy's really wasting away, makes you wanna c-c-cry...'

At her round table, the enchanting Nadezhda Adelheim as usual presided over a cultivated discussion of art, and treated us to some remarkable puff-pastry pies and such pork cutlets as would have made How-Much-fer-Salt feel like the luckiest of mortals.

I handed my plate back to her.

She was amazed:

'Anatoly, are you ill?'

Half a cutlet remained untouched (and this was in 1919).

1919 was the worst year of War Communism, economic dislocation and food shortages.

'No... I'm all right.'

George Yakulov even broke off a tirade on his *Horse Race*, turned his downy lashes on me and, sympathetically flitting his eyes (which resembled the prune pit he'd just plucked out of his mouth) from my plate to my nose, said:

'You should... g-heh, g-heh... Anatoly, you should either... g-heh, g-heh... go lie down... or drink some vodka.'

Yakulov, see p. 23

Esenin patted him on the shoulder:

'Shall we have seconds, George?'

'Certainly, Seryozha... g-heh, g-heh... Certainly. As I was saying... when those snivelers were still painting flowers in vases, Serov declared, after standing for an hour in front of my *Horse Race*, g-heh, g-heh...'

Valentin Serov (1865-1911) Russian Impressionist painter, belonged to the 'World of Art' association.

3—4666

'I know, George.'

'Well, there you are, my dear man, I've already told you... g-heh, g-heh... some fifty times... and I'll tell you a hundred times yet... g-heh, g-heh... that all those Frenchmen... g-heh, g-heh... your Picasso, Matisse... and those sundry stage directors there... g-heh... g-heh... Tairov with his town squares... g-heh, g-heh... all those *Salomes* g-heh, g-heh... even the undisputed genius of Meyerhold, my dear man, — they all came from my *Horse Race. Horse Race*, yes, sir! The entire Jack of Diamonds, too, my dear man...'

Alexander Tairov (1885-1950) avant-garde stage director, founder of the Kamerny Theatre in 1914.

'Jack of Diamonds' (*Bubnovy Valet*), an association of Moscow artists in 1910-16, working in the manner of the Fauvists with elements of Russian folk art.

My heart ached. Poor How-Much-fer-Salt! Here in this tragic moment, when your brow blazes its rage down upon us like a torch; when for you the whole world is painted in the black hues of perfidy, parsimony and conceit; when the glow of that tender and wonderful word, 'friendship,' has forever darkened in your eyes, turned into a greasy candle-end, smoking fumes of betrayal and heartlessness — in this moment, he whom you called your best friend is polishing off his second pork cutlet and carrying on these exceptional, paradoxical discourses on the beautiful.

Ten days later Esenin and I were standing on a platform at the Kazan Station, gray with sacks, bags and gloom. How-Much-fer-Salt was leaving for Turkestan in a separate carriage (on soft springs), accompanied by a secretary, wearing a spiked helmet with a red star the size of a palm, and an assistant with a huge revolver in a yellow holster.

Embracing Molabukh and kissing him fondly on the lips, I said:

'You silly fool, go on and thank Sergei for putting you back on your feet.'

They kissed long and ardently, spicing their smacks with warm profanity and grunts, the sort that only butchers make when they plunge an axe into the carcass of a bull.

21

Our secret electric heater was discovered. For days, Esenin and I lived in fear. We speculated for hours on end as to what punishment Revolutionary law would bring down on our heads. We had nightmares about Lubyanka, an investigator with hawk-like eyes, black steel bars. When our house committee amnestied our crime, we had a feast. Friends shook our hands, girlfriends cried tears of joy, they all embraced and congratulated us on this unexpected outcome. In celebration we drank tea from a samovar brought to a boil by St. Nicholas: we had no coal or chips — so we had to chop up this old icon, hanging humbly in the corner of the room. Only How-Much-fer-Salt refused to drink the divine tea. He pushed away the seductively steaming glass, sat sullenly, and angrily explained that his grandfather was a believer, that he had great respect for his grandfather and just three years ago such tea would have gotten us all exiled to Siberia.

Meanwhile, the winter was becoming fiercer by the week.

After the mishap with the electric heater, we decided to remove to our tiny bathroom, thus giving up a writing desk of seasoned oak wood, a superlative set of bookshelves along with the complete collected works of our landlord Karp Karpovich and the enviable spaciousness of our ice-cold study.

We covered the bathtub with a mattress for a bed; the washstand with boards for a desk; and the little water heater tank we fueled with books.

The warmth from the water heater inspired us to compose lyrical verses.

A few days after our move to the bathroom Esenin read to me:

The astral belfry bangs away in silence,
Every leaf is a candle to the dawn,
I'll let no one in my chamber,
To no one will I open the door.

And indeed: we were forced to defend our discovery, the 'Promised Bathroom', tooth and nail as well as with a heavy lock. The neighbors in our communal apartment, envious of our warm, carefree existence, held meetings and passed resolutions, demanding that turns be taken for residence by the water heater pipe and that we, who had seized a shared space without the proper warrant, be evicted.

We were implacable and hard as stone.

Shortly after New Year's Eve I began squiring a girl. Esenin made a fuss over this; he would knit his brows when I disappeared in the evening. Kusikov would add fuel to the fire, hinting that I had betrayed Esenin's friendship. He assured him that it always started that way — with a small infatuation, and ended ... and here he sang out in his pleasant and supposedly warm-hearted voice:

> *Annoying, vexing*
> *To tears, to torture...*

Esenin knew Kusikov well; he knew that he was like that muzhik in Chekhov's story, who would tell a peasant carting a log, 'Hey, them there logs are deadwood, they're all rotten'; who would tell a fisherman sitting with his rod, 'They ain't a-gonna bite in this weather'; who would assure peasants during a drought, 'There won't be no rain right up 'til the frost comes'; and then when it rained, 'Well, now everything's gonna rot in the fields.'

All the same Esenin was unnerved and distressed by Kusikov's 'Annoying, vexing...'

Once I spent the night out. I came back to our 'Promised Bathroom' around ten in the morning; Esenin was sleeping. On the washstand stood an empty bottle and glass. I had a sniff — the smell of raw vodka seared my nostrils.

I shook Esenin. He raised his heavy, red lids to me.

'What's this, Seryozha? You drank vodka by yourself?'

'Yeah. That's right. An' I'm gonna drink it every day ... if you start spending every night out... look, you can fool around out there with whoever you want, but just come home to sleep.'

That was his rule: he loved to dally, but come four or five in the morning he'd be in his own bed.

We laughed:

'Vyatka's running back into his stall.'

The fundamental thing about Esenin was his fear of being alone.

His last days in the Angleterre Hotel, he would flee his room at night and sit alone in the hall until the sparse winter dawn. On his last night he knocked on the door of Ustinov's room, begging to be let in.

The Angleterre is the hotel in St Petersburg where Esenin committed suicide in December 1925.

Georgy Ustinov (1888-1932) Bolshevik journalist, editor of *Soviet Land*, a newspaper where Esenin published his verse. Committed suicide.

22

By the end of winter we had lost our fortress. We were forced to retreat from the bathroom — back to the icy expanses of our room.

Esenin and I started sleeping in the same bed. We'd pile a mountain of blankets and coats on top of ourselves. On the even days of the month I'd be the one to contort myself first on the ice-cold linen, heating it with my breath and body warmth. On the odd days Esenin did it.

A poetess asked Esenin to help her find a job. She had rosy cheeks, round hips and plump shoulders.

Esenin said he could set her up as a Soviet typist if she would come round to our place every night about one o'clock, disrobe and crawl in between our frigid sheets. It wouldn't take her fifteen minutes to warm the bed! Then she could crawl out, dress and go home.

He promised that we would be sitting with our backs to her throughout, our noses buried in manuscripts.

For three days, precisely observing these conditions, we lay down to sleep in a poetess-warmed bed.

On the fourth day our poetess gave notice, her voice choked with indignation, her pupils round with rage, turning her eyes from sky-blue to black, like the buttons on our lacquered boots.

We were perplexed:

'What's wrong? We observed the conditions religiously...'

'That's just it!' she said. 'I didn't hire myself out to warm the beds of saints.'

'Oh!'

But it was too late: the door slammed so hard in my face that all six screws in the English lock popped out of their holes.

23

Of those responsible for Esenin's notorious hooliganism, first place goes to the critics, then the readership, and then the crowds that crammed the halls of the literary evenings, literary cafes and clubs.

Even before the shock tactics of the Imagists, in the time of *Otherland* and *Transfiguration*, the press had tossed out this word at him — 'hooligan' — and it stuck to him like a nickname or stock epithet; it was drummed into people's minds with astonishing regularity.

Otherland and *Transfiguration*, two long poems, published in 1918, welcomed the Revolution as social and spiritual transformation.

The critics advised Esenin to cultivate his hooligan reputation, to play the hooligan in his verse and in his life.

I remember a critical note that served as the impetus for the writing of the poem '*Light rain cleanses with wet brooms*,' in which he first exclaimed in verse:

Spit, you wind, leaves by the armful,
Just like you, I am a hooligan.

Esenin read this piece to great acclaim. When he walked onto the stage, the crowd would wail:

'Hooligan!'

He decided then — with absolute sobriety and detachment, with his rational mind — that this was his path, his 'shirt.'

Esenin bound his own poetic tendrils and those of everyday life into one wreath.

'That kind of broom is better,' he would say.

And with it he swept the way clear to glory.

I don't know which Esenin transfigured more often: his life into poetry or his poetry into life.

A mask was becoming his face, and his face the mask.

His long poem *Confessions of a Hooligan* soon appeared, and on its heels the book of the same name, shortly followed by *Moscow of the Taverns*, *The Love of a Hooligan*, etc., in every possible variation.

Thus did St Peter turn Jesus into Christ.

Near Caesarea Philippi Jesus asked his apostles:

'Whom do men say that I am?'

They spoke of the rumors in Galilee: some said he was the resurrected John the Baptist, others Elijah, still others Jeremiah or one of the prophets.

Then Jesus asked the apostles:

'But whom say ye that I am?'

Peter answered:

'Thou art the Christ.'

For the first time Jesus did not reject this title.

The conviction of his simple-minded apostles, about whose lack of enlightenment he'd had cause to complain more than once, confirmed Jesus in his decision to play the part of Christ, the anointed one.

Once, when Esenin, in a fit of temper, shoved Isadora Duncan (who'd been pressing up against him) roughly aside, she fervently cried out:

'Russian love!'

Esenin, his brows slyly devouring his gray eyes, understood immediately what this woman appreciated most in his feelings towards her.

It's the most unbelievable nonsense, that art ennobles the soul.

According to Greek literature, the son-and-wife-killing Herod, ruler of Judea and disciple of Nicholas of Damascus, was one of the most hard-hearted figures humanity has ever known. Nonetheless, architectural monuments in Biblos, Baritos, Tripolis, Ptolemy, Damascus, and even in Athens and Sparta bear witness to his love of the beautiful. He adorned pagan temples with sculptures. The Askalon fountains and bathhouses, and the Antioch porticos running along the major thoroughfares — all built during Herod's reign — transported one to raptures. Jerusalem has Herod to thank for its theater and hippodrome. He provoked the guile of Rome for turning Judea into a satellite of the imperial sun.

In none of Esenin's poems do you find such lyrical warmth, such sadness and pain, as in those he wrote in his final years — the years filled with the black terror of drunkenness, emotional disintegration and bitterness.

Once, in the middle of reciting a poem, he grabbed a heavy beer mug and hit Ivan Pribludny, his true

Ivan Pribludny (real name Yakov Ovcharenko, 1905-1937) poet. Grew up in an orphange, fought in the Revolution and the Civil War. Imitated Esenin. Executed as an 'enemy of the people.'

Leporello, on the head. His motive was so trivial it's escaped my memory. Gushing blood, his head cut, Pribludny was taken to the hospital.

Somebody shot out:

'And what if he dies, what then?'

Without batting an eye Esenin said:

'We'll have one dog less to worry about!'

24

Strictly speaking, our partners' investment in the bookshop was a complete waste of money.

A flustered David Samoilovich Eisenstadt, the head, heart and golden hands of our 'business', would appeal to Esenin:

'It would be better, Sergei Alexandrovich, for you not to wait on customers at all than to wait on them the way you and Anatoly Borisovich do.'

This was regarding a man who had dropped into the shop and asked:

'Do you have Mayakovsky's *A Cloud in Trousers*?'

Esenin had retreated a step or two, narrowed his eyes to slits as if sizing the man up, first from head to foot, then from ear to ear, and, after a contemptuous pause, replied in an icy voice:

'Perhaps you would like, my good sir, to take some Nadson off our hands? We have an elegant edition bound in morocco and embossed with gold.'

The customer was insulted:

'And just why Nadson, comrade?'

'Why, because I consider it all the same crap! Going from one to the other you neither gain nor lose in poetic

David Eisenstadt (1880-1947) bookseller, opened a bookshop in 1919 together with Esenin, Mariengof and Kozhebatkin.

Vladimir Mayakovsky (1893-1930) major Russian poet. Started as a Futurist and later became the leading poet of the Revolution. Committed suicide.

Semyon Nadson (1862-1887) a mediocre poet.

dignity. The cover of Mr. Nadson's book, though, is incomparably superior.'

Blushing like an anise apple, the customer cleared out of the shop.

A satisfied Esenin, his face to the books and his back to the counter, plucked a more appetizing volume from the shelf, tenderly tapped its spine, patted its cover as if it were a horse's neck, and turned to the last page:

'Three hundred and twenty.'

He stood there silently moving his lips, adding something up, then he burst into a smile, his eyes radiant: 'So, if all my verse is collected in a book like this, then I'll take up, let's say, 320 pages.'

'What!'

'Well, 160.'

When it came to numbers, Esenin was capable of all sorts of exaggeration, but he was quite compliant. Talking once about his amorous conquests, he went off:

'In fact, Anatoly, in all my life I've had maybe 3,000 women.'

'Vyatka, don't lie.'

'Well, 300.'

'Oho!'

'Well, 30.'

'That's more like it.'

Our other partner in the bookshop was Alexander Kozhebatkin, a man sketched with a sharp pencil and in a style all his own.

Alexander Kozhebatkin (1884-1942) publisher.

In the years of the Decadents he worked at the Musagette Press, then ran his own magazine *Halcyone*, collected Pushkin-era poets and, unlike most of the world's bibliophiles, often read beyond the first page of a book. He loved not just old vignettes, the ancient smell of dusty books, the publishing date and yellowing paper, but the authors themselves.

He would come to the shop, fish a bottle of red wine out of his shabby briefcase and, leaving 'Dosya' (David Samoilovich) to tend to the customers, he'd split the bottle with us in the back room.

Anton Delvig (1798-1831) poet. Pushkin's classmate and close friend.

After the second glass he'd usually quote a line from Pushkin, Delvig or Baratynsky:

Evgeny Baratynsky (1800-1844) poet, Pushkin's rival.

'Where's this from, sir poets?'

Esenin thoughtfully pondered the riddle:

'From Kusikov!'

Kozhebatkin looked pleased. He'd pour out another round, finishing the bottle.

Then, triumphantly:

'We're la-a-a-azy and uninqui-i-i-sitive!'

A quote from Pushkin.

Kozhebatkin's worldly wisdom was simple:

'Business will stay put, but a good conversation over a bottle of wine is hard to duplicate.'

Even while the shop still existed, paintings and rare engravings started disappearing from the walls of his apartment. Then the books on his shelves began thinning out.

It so happened that I hadn't been to his place in about a year. When I finally dropped by, my heart drew in its tail and whined inside my chest: an empty bookcase in the home of a bibliophile is like a corpse in the house.

Finally there was room to breathe at Kozhebatkin's:

the bookcases had been inventoried by the bailiff, carted away and sold at auction.

When the somber funeral procession carrying the coffin of the king of Spain approaches the stone Escorial and the marshal knocks on the gate, a monk asks:

'Who's there?'

'He who was king of Spain,' answers a voice from the procession.

The heavy gate opens before the dead body that 'speaks.'

The monk in the Escorial is obliged to believe that this is the king's own voice. Such is the etiquette.

When the printers call Kozhebatkin, asking him to come immediately and approve the proofs of some urgent book, and at the same time George Yakulov suggests they split a bottle, romantic 'etiquette' obliges Kozhebatkin to trust his worldly wisdom that 'business will stay put', and make his way to some nice Georgian restaurant.

The next day the printers' bill would have doubled, due to the press having had to 'stand idle.'

25

In early spring we moved out of Bogoslovsky into the small apartment of Semyon Bystrov on Georgievsky Lane near Patriarch's Ponds. Bystrov worked at our shop, too.

And so began our carefree existence.

Cozy little rooms with low ceilings, tiny windows; a cozy kitchenette with a huge Russian stove, cheap wallpaper like it was made out of provincial chintz, a pot-bellied chest of drawers, the classics supplement to the *Niva* magazine in those colorful *Niva* covers. What joy!

It was like being back in my dear Penza, or Esenin's Ryazan.

That we might live without a care in the world, our dear solicitous host found us (ach, the joker!) a housemaid.

The fetching lass had turned 93 in February.

'She is a maiden,' he informed us just in case. 'She asked me to let you know.'

'Fine. Fine. Our manners in regards to her maiden virtue shall be without reproach.'

'Very good.'

We took to calling our maiden 'Granny Housemaid,' while she called us 'the black one' and 'the white one.'

She would complain about us to Bystrov:

'The white one brought in another one today.'

'Whom did he bring in, grandma?'

'Pfoo! To say it would be indecent...'

'She must be an acquaintance of his, grandma.'

'Pfoo! Pfoo! She's shameless, coming to see a man all by herself. You'd think she'd at least be ashamed in front of me, a maiden.'

Or:

'Be a good boy, dear, and tell the black one not to sprinkle himself with flour.'

'What flour, grandma?'

He knew it had in fact been face powder.

'It makes me sick to watch him: he sprinkles flour on his nose. He's floured the whole floor. You're sweeping it up! You're sweeping it up!'

Every time we came home, we'd press the doorbell with trepidation lest there be no one home to open the door — lest we find the unbreathing corpse of our granny-maiden lying there.

But no: we could hear her shuffling her leathery heels, wheezing, turning the key. And we'd feel relieved till the next day.

Once we were robbed dry. They took everything: our coats and even our suits and shoes. It was no laughing matter in those years. Where would we ever find replacements?

We lay in our beds, blacker than storm clouds.

Suddenly we heard granny wheezing at the door.

She had a tragic look on her face:

'They stole my co-o-o-oat.'

And Esenin said in the same tone:

'D'ja hear that, Tolya? They stole granny's trousseau right out of her trunk.'

And, turning over onto our stomachs, burying our faces in the pillows, we started rolling in the most indecent laughter, considering those perfidious circumstances.

Bystrov's housekeeping, the naivete of the little apartment, the tranquility of Georgievsky Lane and the romantic air of our housemaid were all conducive to creativity.

We spent a lot of time with our verse and developing our theories of Imagism.

I don't know where that unfinished manuscript of Esenin's vanished to. My *Buyan-Island* was published by Kozhebatkin that autumn.

Mariengof's *Buyan-Island* (1920) was one of the fundamental texts of Imagist poetics.

The work on our theory led us into the fantastic labyrinth of philology.

We indulged in our homespun science of laying bare and bringing to light the strange, at times fundamental, imagistic roots and stems of words.

Sometimes I'd just be tearing myself away from sleep, and Esenin would yell:

'Anatoly, *krysa* (rat).'

I'd answer in a drowsy voice:

'*Gryst*' (gnaw).'

'Right, now make something from a root.'

'*Ozero* (lake), *zrak* (vision).'

'It's neat to go from image to root, too; *ruka* (hand) *ruchei* (stream), *reka* (river) *rech* (speech)...'

'*Krylo* (wing) *kryltso* (porch)...'

'*Oko* (eye) *okno* (window)...'

Once, archly knitting his brows, he challenged me:

'Go on, make something out of *sor* (rubbish).'

And, without giving me a chance to think, he said triumphantly:

'*Sortir* (toilet).'

'Ach, come on, Vyatka, but *sortir* is a French word.'

Esenin was extremely offended. He pouted all evening long.

It seemed to us that once we'd proven the imagistic evolution of language from its infancy, our theory would be irrefutable.

Poetry is like a patchwork village blanket, made from a multitude of many-colored scraps. But we focussed on one of them to the exclusion of all else.

We were not unlike the village priest who was

obsessed with the idea of iodine. He'd conceived an ineluctable faith in its panacean powers.

One day the priest's wife, wiping the dust from a closet, happened to overturn his large bottle of iodine. It spread across the floor like melted copper.

The priest cried out:

'Ach, Lord Jesus! What a disaster, Lord Jesus!'

With that, he pulled down his pants and lifted his cassock and planted his ample buttocks in the puddle of iodine:

'So that this boon, Lord Jesus, not go to waste!'

He invited his wife to join him.

'You sit down, too, Martha Petrovna, suck the blessing in through your organs!'

You may laugh but here is another good example.

I'm standing on Akulov Hill in Pushkino, my two-year-old son Kirill on my shoulders, gazing at the fiery-red setting sun.

Pushkino is a resort town near Moscow.

Kirill stretches out his little hand towards the sunset and says, beaming:

Mariengof's only son Kirill committed suicide at the age of 17 for no apparent reason.

'Ball.'

He looks some more and, shaking his tiny head, changes his mind:

'Balloon.'

At last, grabbing me hard by the nose he decides, quite assured of his guess:

'No. A clock.'

What vivid images! What splendid visual aids corroborating the manner in which words form.

26

Bystrov's children lived somewhere in Tambov province. He was thinking of moving them to Moscow, so he started looking for another place for us.

He said that just down Georgievsky Lane the Prince and Princess V. were ready to take in lodgers to avoid having any of their rooms taken away from them by the State.

The prince warned Bystrov:

'No Jews or Bolsheviks.'

The next day we set out to inspect this 'tranquil haven,' as Bystrov described it.

The prince was past sixty, the princess just about there, and both were small, neat and gray. The little room was not unlike them. Esenin and I immediately took a fancy to it.

We were just a bit surprised to see the little chamber furnished with some fifteen tables of every size and shape: round, oval, card tables, tea tables, tables of ebony, mahogany, Karelian birch, some special kind of walnut, pearl-inlaid tables, wood-inlaid tables — in a word, you couldn't enumerate all the different kinds.

Esenin asked in a most humble tone:

'Would it be possible to take maybe five tables out of the room?'

The prince and princess were insulted. They angrily shook their heads.

We had to resign ourselves to the tables and started saying our goodbyes. The prince, extending his hand, asked us:

'So, this means you're going to live here?'

But instead of *zhit* (to live), Esenin heard *zhid* (yid).

He said in alarm:

'What are you saying, prince, I'm not a yid... I'm not a yid...'

The prince and princess looked at each other. Sparks of distrust glittering in their little eyes.

They slammed the door after us.

In the morning, over tea, Bystrov relayed the princely couple's answer: 'the redhead' (Esenin) was undoubtedly a Jew and a Bolshevik, and 'the tall one,' looked suspicious, too — not for any money would they allow us to live in their house.

The astonished Esenin almost swallowed his cup.

27

During the spring thaw we prepared to go to Kharkov. Every man in Moscow then was secretly yearning for white Ukrainian bread, lard, sugar, so that his belly could work like a mill in autumn — at least for a week or two.

My old nanny used to say about Moscow:

'What a life! Nothing to eat and nothing to pass.'

For the last month Esenin had been winning at cards. He was saving up money for the journey.

At first we'd both sit at the card table — I lost, he won.

At daybreak we'd compare our wallets: one fat, the other empty.

Counting up the money, we found we'd merely broken even.

Esenin said:

'Anatoly, you stay home. This isn't a game, it's a disaster. We're just wasting our nights.'

He started going alone.

He was a dangerous player.

When he won a game he'd never leave the money on the table. He'd put it in all his various pockets: trousers, vest, jacket.

If he started to lose, he would turn out only some of his pockets and say:

'I'm dry.'

His final stakes would be on credit.

He would come home, wake me up and empty crisp notes out of his other pockets onto the blanket.

'Here, see? That's how you play!'

On the eve of our trip, Schwartz read his *Gospel According to Judas* at our place on Georgievsky.

Schwartz was a curious person, of great learning, cultivated, and an original thinker. A brilliant associate professor at Moscow University, he preached an inspiringly cynical apology of middle-class values. In the geranium, the canary and the gramophone he saw the happy future of humankind. When the tastes of some rose to an appreciation, to an absolute need for a little rose on their window sill, while the refinement of others descended to the level of a little yellow bird's trilling, the Golden Age would arrive.

On stage, Schwartz was always entertaining, caustic and witty.

How unjust that this small black figure, with a perfectly round, pale head, a monocle on a thick cord ever in one eye, has gone, leaving behind not a trace of itself. He resembled an ebony cane with an ivory knob for a handle.

Schwartz had spent twelve years writing his *Gospel According to Judas.*

He decided to read it first to us — the youngest, most 'leftist' and most cavalier towards the gods and idols of literature.

He explained:

'I need noses. So they can sniff out whether this meat has a stench or not. For this purpose, your noses are the most suitable.'

We invited Kozhebatkin and two or three other friends to the reading.

Schwartz's *Gospel* was not a success.

Apparently he had expected those three typewritten pages, the fruit of twelve years of labor, to have the impact of *War and Peace.*

Schwartz finished reading in such a state of agitation the monocle popped out of his eye.

Esenin placed a friendly hand on his knee:

'You know, Schwartz, it's cra-a-a-ap! You're such an independent-minded man, but in front of Jesus you're like some innocent little girl bobbing and curtsying. Remember what the Pharisees said about Jesus to his disciples: "How is it that he eateth and drinketh with publicans and sinners?" That's how you should have gone about it. You could have made something out of an image like that. But instead you give us treacle ... and call it "according to Judas." '

Waving his hand in a gesture of helplessness, Esenin broke into a tender smile.

N.L.Schwartz did not shoot himself that night but died a month later from an overdose of cocaine.

That night Schwartz shot himself.

We learned of his death the following morning.

Our train was leaving at four. We wanted to escape Moscow, to stop up our ears with our fists and smother our brains.

We met up with friends at the station. The iron stove crackled merrily in the heated goods van. Red Army soldiers were riding in the next carriage. They started bawling songs and cracking jokes. One of them, blue-eyed, with high cheekbones, nostrils like a turnpike, and a soft, plump mouth, played the accordion marvelously.

At some station along the way I was still standing in line to get some hot water when the train started moving. Hurrying back, I jumped onto the Red Army soldiers' carriage.

Nearing Tula, the train speeded up.

A large white dog raced along the embankment, happily wagging its tail.

The blue-eyed soldier set aside the accordion and, raising his rifle, fired.

The dog, which just now had been happily wagging its tail, sank to the ground nosefirst. Its white paws flashed in the air, then it rolled down the embankment into a ditch.

Satisfied with his shot, the Red soldier turned to me, his soft face, with its high cheekbones and plump mouth breaking into a good-natured smile:

'Thas the way...'

One more smile, just like that one, sticks in my mind like a thorn.

A plumber lived in our courtyard. His wife had died of typhus. He was left with a hapless little boy of five, practically an idiot.

The plumber kept going round to various agencies and orphanages, hoping to place the boy.

Each time I ran into him, I'd ask:

'Well, so how goes it — did you manage to place Volodya?'

'They said: "in the near future." '

The next week he reported:

'They asked me to come back in a week.'

Or:

'They said I oughta wait a little.'

And so on and so forth.

At last I heard a different answer from the plumber:

'I placed him, Anatoly, I placed my Volodya.'

And with the very same gentle smile — so familiar to me — he told me how he'd 'placed' him. He'd bought a ticket at Yaroslavsky railway station, boarded the train with Volodya, and at Sergiev Posad, when the child had dozed off, he slipped out of the carriage and took the return train to Moscow.

Volodya went on alone.

28

We're strolling along Sumskaya Street in Kharkov, Esenin in a fur coat, I in an overcoat of thick English wool, while the local young people are strutting about in just their jackets.

Esenin is holding a note with the address of Lev Povitsky, a good friend of his.

Lev Povitsky (1890-1969), journalist. Esenin also stayed with him in Batumi, Georgia. Povitsky published Esenin's verse in his newspaper *Working Batumi.*

Sergei Klychkov (1889-1940) peasant poet. Executed as 'an enemy of the people.'

In 1918 Povitsky had lived in Tula with his brother who worked in a brewery. Esenin and Sergei Klychkov had stayed with them for quite a while and had a very good time.

Afterwards they often recalled that visit, and invariably with great pleasure.

With Povitsky's help we counted on finding food and lodging.

We asked the way of passers-by.

A boot-black was putting a stunning shine on somebody's box-calf shoes with a velvet cloth.

'I'll go ask that fop how to get there.'

'Go ahead.'

'Pardon me, comrade...'

The comrade turned toward the voice and, leaving the puzzled boot-black holding his velvet cloth, fell on Esenin with open arms:

'Seryozha!'

'You're just the man we're looking for, you devil. Mariengof, meet Povitsky.'

Povitsky took us to his friends' place, promising love and hospitality. He himself was staying with somebody else.

We passed a tiny street, crossed two or three alleys.

'You go in, Lev, and make inquiries. If they're agreeable call out to us, otherwise we'll turn back.'

In less than a minute half a dozen girls, chirping and squealing, had darted out to meet us.

Povitsky was pleased.

'What'd I say? Eh?'

They dragged a table out of an enormous dining

room and put a double-sized hair mattress on the floor in its place.

It was as if they'd known us both for years, as if the mattress had been kept in store for just this purpose, and the dining room had been meant precisely for this occasion.

There are indeed kind people in this world!

We had traveled eight days from Moscow to Kharkov; at night we stoked the stove in shifts; when we slept, we placed a palm under our hip-bone to cushion it.

The girls 'tucked us in' at nine o'clock. We didn't object even for the sake of appearances. Exhaustion shod our eyelids like heavy soldier's boots, or so it seemed.

We awoke — at one o'clock the next afternoon — on the same side we'd fallen asleep on. We hadn't turned over once all night long.

All six girls were walking around on tiptoe.

The spring sun leaned its hot palm on our dark curtain.

Esenin lay with his back to me.

I started running my fingers through his hair.

'What're you digging in there for?'

'Ooh, Vyatka, you're in trouble. You have a bald spot the size of a silver five-ruble piece.'

'Is that right?' He began inspecting his silver five-ruble piece using two mirrors.

In our robust, daring youth, we loved to hash out things unrelated to our lives — we invented 'January frost in our hair', non-existent 'silver five-ruble pieces', 'autumn coolness in our thick, hot blood'.

Esenin set aside his mirror and reached for a pencil.

A tender, fragile bitterness is as pleasant for the heart as it is for the tongue.

Still in bed, at one stroke, almost without corrections (which he rarely made then in any case), he composed a touching lyrical poem.

An hour later, over breakfast, he was already reading it to the reverently attentive girls:

The owl swoops, autumn-like,
Over the expanse of a road's early hour.
Leaves are falling from my head,
The golden bush of my hair withers.

'Koo-goo' calls in the steppe,
Greetings, mother blue aspen.
Soon the moon, swimming in snow,
Will rest in her son's sparse curls.

Soon I'll be shivering without my leaves,
My ears filling with star ringing.
Youths will be singing without me,
Old men will pay me no heed.

29

Velemir Khlebnikov lived in Kharkov. We decided to call on him.

A very large, square room. In one corner, an iron bed without a mattress or bedding, in another corner a solitary stool. On the stool lay shavings of leather, waxed thread, an old torn sole, a shoe needle and an awl.

Khlebnikov was sitting on the floor and fussing with some rusty, headless nails. He had a boot over his right hand.

Velemir Khlebnikov (1885-1922) a highly original Futurist poet who created 'a new world of words' through his extensive verbal experimentation.

He stood up to greet us, putting out the hand with the boot on it.

Smiling, I 'shook hands' with the boot. Khlebnikov didn't even notice.

Esenin asked:

'What's this, Velemir, you're wearing a boot instead of a glove?'

Khlebnikov looked confused and his ears reddened — thin, long ears, like deflated horns.

'Well... I stitch my boots myself. Have a seat...'

We sat on the bed.

'Well...'

He took in the bare quadrangle of his room with his large eyes, gray and clear like the eyes of saints in Dionysi Glushitski's icons.

' ... this room ... it's fine ... it's just I don't like ... too much furniture ... it's superfluous ... gets in the way...'

I thought Khlebnikov was kidding.

But he spoke seriously, pulling at his hair, cut very short after a bout of typhus.

Khlebnikov's head was elongated and greenly diaphanous, bringing to mind a drinking glass.

' ... and I could sleep on the floor ... but I need the stool ... I write on the windowsill instead of ... a desk ... I don't have any kerosene ... so I'm learning to write... a poem ... in the dark ... all last night ...'

He showed us a sheet of paper, covered with scribbles, one on top of the other, grappling with each other, all mixed up. It was impossible to read a single word.

'What, you can actually make this out?'

'No ... I thought I wrote about a hundred lines ... but when it got light ... there it is...'

He eyes became bitter:

'A poem ... a pity, really ... oh, well ... I'll learn to write in the dark...'

Khlebnikov wore a long black frock-coat with silk lapels and canvas pants gathered below the knee into leg-wrappings.

The overcoat's lining doubled as bedding.

Khlebnikov looked at my shiny hair, parted evenly down the middle and smoothed out with a stiff brush.

'Mariengof, I like your hair-do ... I'll have mine done like that too...'

Esenin said:

'Velemir, you are indeed the "Chairman of the Globe." We want to publicly declare your election in a gala ceremony at the Kharkov City Theater.'

Khlebnikov gratefully shook our hands.

A week later the ritual was performed for a thousand-eyed gathering.

Khlebnikov, in a sack-cloth cassock, barefoot, his hands crossed on his chest, listened to Esenin and I read doxologies consecrating him as 'Chairman.'

At the end of each quatrain, as we'd agreed, he intoned:

'I believe.'

He said 'I believe' so quietly we could barely hear him. Esenin poked him:

'Velemir, speak louder. The audience can't hear a damn thing.'

Khlebnikov raised his uncomprehending eyes, as if to ask: 'But what's an audience doing here?'

And he said 'I believe' even more quietly, only mouthing the words.

In conclusion, as a symbol of the 'Globe,' we placed a ring on his finger, one borrowed from the evening's fourth participant, Boris Glubokovsky.

Boris Glubokovsky, actor at the Kamerny Theatre and Imagist writer. Arrested in 1920, committed suicide in prison camp.

The curtain fell.

Glubokovsky walked over to Khlebnikov:

'Velemir, give me my ring back.'

Khlebnikov looked at him in alarm and hid his hand behind his back.

Glubokovsky got mad:

'Stop playing the fool, give me the ring!'

Esenin was convulsed with laughter.

Khlebnikov's lips were white:

'This ... this ... "Globe" ... It's a symbol of the "Globe" ... And I — look ... They consecrated me ... Esenin and Mariengof ... as "Chairman"...'

Glubokovsky, out of patience, tore the ring right off his finger.

The Chairman of the Globe broke into tears, burying his face in the dusty wings, big, horse-like tears rolling down his face.

Before returning to Moscow we published a small collection, *The Tavern of Dawn*, in Kharkov.

Esenin contributed his *Mare Ships*, I my *I Shall Meet*, and Khlebnikov a long poem and some short verse:

The Golgotha
of Mariengof.
The city
Unstitched.
The Resurrection
of Esenin.
My lord, go calve
In a coat of fox.

30

On Easter night on a Kharkov boulevard, paved with a thronging crowd, we read our verse.

Esenin recited his *Pantokrator.*

In his high voice, he wedged his words between the din of church bells:

It wasn't to pray to you
that you taught me, oh Lord,
But to bark at you.

The crowd, in pointed cloth helmets, hats and peaked caps, contracted into a huge black fist. Esenin dropped the words like heavy copper coins on the asphalt.

And for the sake of these hoary curls,
For these kopecks from gilded aspen,
I scream, 'To hell with everything Old',
I, your disobedient hooligan son.

When Esenin finished the cloth helmets and peaked caps raised him up and began throwing him into the air, into the Easter night, to the din of church bells.

A good test for one's verse.

It went even better for Gogol.

The old Bolshevik M. Vainstein recounted the following incident to me:

When he was imprisoned in the Peter and Paul Fortress, the cell next to his was occupied by a maximalist whose trial was in its final days. The prison expected a death sentence. The air grew hard as rock, and the thoughts in Vainstein's head moved sluggishly, heavily, like fattened swine.

Suddenly: from the maximalist's cell, through the thick Peter and Paul walls there came the sound of rollicking laughter, the kind that comes from the heart. Laughter before the gallows is more horrifying than sobs.

Vainstein raised the alarm; it seemed death had been outstripped by madness.

The overseer came, looked in on the maximalist, spread his hands and shook his head in puzzlement:

'He's reading.'

Using the Morse code, Vainstein knocked on the wall: 'What's the matter?'

The maximalist replied:

'I'm reading Gogol. *Christmas Eve*. About the blacksmith Vakula. I can't help it, it's so funny...'

31

Of all printed matter, the stuff we liked the least was that produced by the Military Commissariat. At first we'd carefully read all the mobilization orders. We'd read them and fret. We felt the flimsiness of our immunity papers. Finally, as a more reassuring measure, we stopped reading any mobilization orders at all. We'd just dash past the freshly-posted orders in even greater haste.

We'd close our eyes to them, but the announcements started creeping into our ears.

In his fright, Esenin went to see the Commissar of Circuses, Nina Rukavishnikova.

Circus performers were exempted from the duty and honor of defending the Soviet republic with rifle in hand.

Rukavishnikova proposed that Esenin ride out into the ring on horseback and recite some poetic nonsense to accompany a bit of pantomime.

For three days, Esenin pranced about on horseback, while some girls and I backed him up with thunderous applause from the stalls.

His fourth performance proved less successful.

Something was tickling the circus jade's nostril and she shook her head so violently that Esenin, who had grown used to her quiet disposition, flew out of his saddle, somersaulted through the air, and wound up sprawled on the ground.

'I'll be better off forfeiting my head in honest battle,' he told Rukavishnikova.

By mutual consent their six-month contract was cancelled.

The next day How-Much-fer-Salt arrived from Turkestan. That evening we split a bottle of sultana wine at the house of a friend. It was very late when the three of us left.

On the street we continued to bawl about the 'strange twists of love.'

Turkestan — from 1919 to 1924, an autonomous republic within the Russian Federation. Occupied the whole of Central Asia with a capital in Tashkent. Later split into Uzbekistan, Tajikistan, Turkmenistan, and Kirgizia

Esenin had brought back with him from Kharkov some tender feelings for an 18-year-old girl with 'Biblical' eyes. This girl loved poetry. From early evening until daybreak they'd sit in an unhitched gig, in the middle of the small round courtyard, the girl gazing at the moon, Esenin at her Biblical eyes.

They discussed the preeminence of imperfect and perfect rhymes, the unseemliness of verb rhymes, the percussion effect of compound rhymes and the pleasing quality of truncated rhymes.

He even started affectionately calling her 'My Little Rhyme.'

Shouting at the top of his lungs, Esenin demanded that I confirm for How-Much-fer-Salt his Little Rhyme's resemblance to King Solomon's love, the beautiful Shulamite.

To get his goat, I said she was as beautiful as any Jewish girl from the shtetl come to Kharkov to take a dentistry course.

Esenin praised her Biblical eyes, I her future agility with a drill.

Suddenly, in the midst of our debate we heard a piercing whistle and saw some Red Militiamen emerge from round the lighted corner.

Esenin exhaled from deep inside his chest:

'Manhunt!'

Only yesterday he'd returned Rukavishnikova's circus certificate of 'immunity.'

We didn't have long to make a decision.

'Run?'

'Run.'

We took to our heels. Behind us whistles rang out, heavy boots thumped and clumped.

How-Much-fer-Salt kept up for twenty paces or so. His back and his knee ached, his cap flew off his head, and papers, like birds quitting a dovecote, fluttered out of his yawning briefcase.

He collapsed on the pavement, his head in his hands.

Cutting a corner, we saw the militiamen arrest him and take him away while the distance between us and our pursuers steadily grew.

In Granatny Lane, Esenin dove inside a black, unfamiliar gate, but I kept running. The occasional nocturnal passerby darted out of my way.

Later on Esenin told us how they'd searched the courtyard in which he'd hidden, how he'd heard them issue the command 'to shoot' if they found him, and how he'd stuck his finger between his gums to keep his teeth from chattering.

For an hour we sat up in our beds, waiting for How-Much-fer-Salt.

But he didn't show up 'til ten in the morning. The poor devil had spent the night at the militia station. Not even his military credentials, with their sinister signatures and seals, were of any help.

He cursed us:

'You idiots, why'd you run? Just 'cause 'a you devils, I got lice and not a wink all night. I had to bring around some whore that was stewed to the gills. They pinched my wallet...'

'Well, we've been all right. We slept ... in our soft beds...'

'Here's how much your credentials are worth. And you boasted that you have the right of arrest for up to thirty days! But instead they locked you right up ... pff!'

'There ain't no "pff!" about it. They asked me, "Who was that with you?" an' I says, "The poets Esenin and Mariengof." '

'What'd you tell 'em that for?'

'Well, why should I stew in jail the rest'a my life on account'a you devils?'

'So?'

'So, then they asked, "Why'd they run?" "Because," I says, "they're idiots." Good thing, too, the duty officer happened to be intelligent: "I see," he says. "Imagists." And he let me go without drawin' up a report.'

How-Much-fer-Salt had meant to bring us raisins, dried apricots, rice and jars of various preserves, but near Tula a food-requisitioning detachment took it all, despite the permits he had for the goods.

In the years of War Communism private trade was prohibited, the approaches to the cities were guarded by food-requisitioning detachments, which confiscated agricultural products from the peasants who tried to smuggle them into the cities for sale or barter.

That particular food-requisitioning detachment and its commander, a former Hussar cavalry sergeant-major — red-haired, freckled, with a nose that stuck out like a spur — were infamous throughout Russia for their barbarity.

32

In midsummer How-Much-fer-Salt received orders for the Caucuses.

'We're going with you.'

'Get yer things together.'

An autonomous white railway coach from the

Turkestan transport service. We had a two-person compartment with soft seats. In the whole carriage there were only four passengers and a conductor.

How-Much-fer-Salt's secretary, Vasily Gastev, had been a classmate of mine at the Nizhny Novgorod Noble's Institute. He was the kind of fellow who's always on his toes.

Gastev wore full field dress: right down to the field binoculars. He had some fantastic chevrons on his cuff. How-Much-fer-Salt's 'railroad' rank put him almost on the same footing as an army general, while Gastev was just shy of being a regimental commander. When he appeared before the station duty officer, irritably tapping his revolver's yellow holster and demanding that our carriage be hitched up 'regardless of who's next in line,' he had the officer shaking in his boots.

'Yes, sir! It'll be the very next one.'

With that kind of secretary, we made the trip as far as Rostov at lightning speed. Instead of the then standard fifteen to twenty days we found ourselves on the platform at Rostov on the fifth day.

Gastev was also in charge of our readings.

Rostov, Taganrog, Novocherkassk — cities in the south of Russia. Today it would take about 24 hours to get there by train, or two hours by plane.

Esenin and I read in Rostov and Taganrog. In Novocherkassk, after a crushing article in a local paper, our reading was cancelled — a few hours before it was due to begin.

This time neither Gastev's yellow holster nor his map case nor his Zeiss binoculars did the trick.

The newspaper recounted the most improbable history of Imagism, our rambunctious biographies, and maliciously hinted at the existence of a secret carriage in which we rode everywhere with a military administrator decorated with diamond chevrons and a red star.

How-Much-fer-Salt fell ill thanks to that article.

Having given orders to 'leave with the very next departing train,' he changed into clean undergarments and shirt, and lay down in his compartment — to die.

We tried to calm him, swore that we wouldn't hold any more readings, but to no avail. He stared silently into the distance with a roaming, lucid gaze, as if the gates of some heavenly kingdom had already opened to receive him.

Meanwhile, he took some castor oil before bed.

The train chugged along the Kuban Steppe.

Esenin tied a cord to the empty phial of castor oil and, swinging it around like a chandelier, performed a burial service over How-Much-fer-Salt whose blood froze in superstitious fear. The effect of the ceremony's lofty words and the melody's unhurried gloom might have proved fatal if not for the salutary and timely effects of the castor oil.

Willy-nilly, How-Much-fer-Salt was forced back on his feet.

Then Esenin came up with a new torture. Knowing how much How-Much-fer-Salt loved food and his condition at the time, he walked into his compartment with a plateful of sliced tomatoes, onions, cucumbers and hard-boiled eggs (a dish our friend adored) and, sitting opposite him, began popping one slice after another into his mouth, smacking and licking his lips. How-Much-fer-Salt turned to Esenin with a pleading voice:

'Seryozha, please, go away.'

The lip-smacking grew more frenzied and more trenchant.

'Seryozha, you know how I love tomatoes... My ticker's even startin' to hurt...'

But Esenin was implacable.

Then How-Much-fer-Salt lay back, closed his eyes and wrapped a pillow around his ears.

Esenin leaned over the pillow, raised one of its corners and smacked even louder and more insistently.

How-Much-fer-Salt darted out. Esenin followed him, with the plate. How-Much-fer-Salt grabbed the first object that came to hand and flung it at his tormentor, who dodged it.

Then the victim yelled, menacingly and commandingly:

'Gastev, revolver!'

'But I've already eaten it all.'

And Esenin showed him the empty plate.

We were lounging in our compartment. Esenin had his nose in Flaubert's *Madame Bovary*. Occasionally he would read aloud a page that had particularly delighted him.

Someone started making a merry racket in the train's rear coaches. The uproar spread from carriage to carriage, through all the officers and staff.

We stuck our heads out the window.

On the steppe, a scrawny chestnut colt, scared to death by the locomotive, was tearing up the road alongside our train.

It was quite a stirring sight. Shrieking for all he

was worth, waving his trousers and craning his shaggy golden head, Esenin cheered the racer on. For almost a mile and a half, the horse of flesh ran even with the one of iron. After that the four-legged one fell behind and out of sight.

Esenin was beside himself.

Past Kislovodsk he wrote a letter to the girl in Kharkov for whom he had tender feelings.

It is of more than passing interest. I cite it here:

Dear, dear Zhenya,

For God's sake, don't think I need something of you. I myself don't know why I can't seem to stop reminding you of my existence. There are all sorts of diseases, and they all pass. I think this one will pass, too.

This morning we left Kislovodsk for Baku and, as I looked out the coach window at the Caucasian landscape, I felt uneasy and taut inside. This is my second time in these parts, and I do not at all understand what it is about the place that so struck the people who produced in our minds the images of the Terek river, Mount Kazbek, Daryal Gorge and all the rest. To be honest, I was more impressed with the Caucasus in my native Ryazan province than here. Today I realized how harmful travel is for me. I don't know what I'd do if for some reason I were forced to circle the entire globe. This planet is already so cramped and dull. Certainly, the living make great leaps, like the transition from horse to train, but all this is just more speed or greater heights. One gets the feeling this all went on long ago, and with greater vigor. The only thing that touches me in this process is a wistfulness for that which is disappearing, the precious, the aboriginal, the feral, everything not capable of withstanding these invincible yet dead mechanical forces.

Here's a good example of this for you. We were traveling from Tikhoretskaya to Pyatigorsk, when suddenly we heard shouts. We looked out the window, and what did we see: beside the engine a small colt was gallopping along with all his might. We immediately understood: for some reason, it had taken it into its head to try and overtake the train. He ran a long while, but in the end he grew tired, and at some station they caught him. This episode, insignificant for most people, to me spoke volumes. The horse of iron vanquished the horse of flesh and bone; this little colt was for me a visual, precious and dying image of Russia, the representation of Makhno. In our revolution, both bear a terrible resemblance to this colt: the living force pitted against the iron one.

Nestor Makhno (1884-1934) leader of an anarchist military uprising in the Ukraine. First Makhno and his cavalry army fought against the German occupation, then against the landlords, and during the Civil War against the Bolsheviks. In 1921, Makhno's men were routed by the Red Army while Makhno himself fled to Romania.

Forgive me, my dear, once again, for alarming you. I feel very sad at the moment that history is undergoing a difficult epoch, in which the individual as a living organism is targeted for destruction. Indeed, what's going on is not the socialism I had envisaged at all, but a definite and deliberate one, like some island of St. Helena, stripped of glory, drained of dreams. You feel cooped up if you're truly alive, if you build bridges to the invisible world, for they sever and detonate these bridges from under the feet of future generations. Of course, he for whom this invisible world unfolds, he will see these bridges, moldy by then, but after all it's always sad to build a house that no one will live in, to hollow out a boat no one will sail in.

S. E.

On the trip from Mineralniye Vody to Baku Esenin wrote his greatest poem, *Prayers for the Dead.* The colt that dared to pit itself against our train was compressed into an image full of meaning and a profoundly disquieting lyricism.

Pyatigorsk, Kislovodsk, Mineralniye Vody — resort towns in the Northern Caucasus. Baku is the capital of Azerbaidzhan. Derbent is a town on the Caspian sea

In Derbent our conductor, drawing water from a well, lost his grip on the bucket and released it forever into the shaft. Esenin made use of this bucket, too, in his address to the iron guest in *Prayers for the Dead*:

A pity that in your infancy
You were not drowned
Like a pail in a well-shaft.

In the port at Petrovsk there was an entire train full of people sick with malaria. We witnessed some truly horrific seizures. People bounced on the planks like rubber balls, gnashed their teeth, bathed in sweat by turns icy and steaming like boiled water.

And in *Prayers for the Dead*:

Lo, a fever of steel shakes
The wooden bellies of huts.

33

I nearly forgot something.

By chance, on the platform at Rostov, I ran into Zinaida Nikolayevna. She was on her way to Kislovodsk.

The previous winter, she had given birth to a boy. She had asked Esenin on the telephone:

'What should we call him?'

Esenin thought for quite some time — trying to pick a non-literary name — and said:

'Konstantin.'

After the christening he suddenly remembered:

'Ah, dammit, Balmont — he's a Konstantin, isn't he.'

Konstantin Balmont (1867-1942) poet who inspired many of the Symbolists.

He didn't go to see his son.

When he saw me talking to Zinaida Nikolayevna on the Rostov platform, Esenin turned on his heels in a perfect semi-circle, jumped onto a rail, and walked away, holding his arms out so as not to lose his balance.

Zinaida Nikolayevna had a request:

'Tell Seryozha I'm traveling with Konstantin. He's never seen him. Let him come have a look. If he doesn't want to meet with me, I can wait outside.'

I headed back to Esenin to convey the message.

At first he would not be moved:

'I'm not going. I don't want to. There's nothing for me to see.'

'Go on — they're about to ring the second warning bell. It's your son, for pity's sake.'

He went into the compartment, knitting his brows. Zinaida Nikolayevna untied the little ribbons of the baby's sleeping bag, made of lace. The tiny pink creature wriggled its little feet.

'Ach! He's got dark hair! None of the Esenins are dark.'

'Seryozha!'

Zinaida Nikolayevna turned away, her shoulders shaking.

'Well, let's go, Anatoly.'

And Esenin, with a light, prancing step, issued out into the corridor of the first-class coach.

34

On the way back to Pyatigorsk we learned of some setbacks in Moscow: it seemed that, in compliance with some order, our book shop and Pegasus' Stall had been closed down, and our books were not being printed though we'd agreed with Kozhebatkin to share the expenses.

I had a tropical fever and was flat on my back. Esenin went back to Moscow alone, on a special Red Army train.

We knocked around another month in the Caucasus. Our coach flitted like a flea between Mineralniye Vody, Petrovsk and Baku.

At last, we were bound for Moscow in the caboose of an express train. The earth seemed all covered over with white bedding, and the mountains, like pillows, stuffed into sparkling linen cases.

In Moscow the first person I ran into was Vadim Shershenevich. I was coming from the station. My head, in a light summer hat, was poking out from under all my suitcases, baskets and sacks.

I had hailed a cab. Shershenevich leaped onto the running board:

'Seryozha's under arrest, you know. He got caught in some raid. Three days ago. But your shop and the Stall are open, and your books are on sale.'

And so, with my suitcases, baskets and sacks, I rushed to the Tsentropechat office instead of home, to Boris Fyodorovich Malkin, our protector and guardian angel.

'What is all this? How on earth can this have happened? What's going on, Boris Fyodorovich? Seryozha's been arrested!'

Malkin picked up the phone.

That evening Esenin was back home. His face was covered with a strange grime, like a gray shadow. His cheeks and chin had sprouted a nice reddish stubble. In his blue eyes, behind the joy, was a profound hurt, gnawing on the affront.

35

We moved back into Bogoslovsky Lane, back into the Bakhrushin house, but a different apartment.

We had three rooms, a maid in a starched lace apron (Emilia), and a Borzoi.

Emilia fed us hazel-grouse, wood-grouse, ice-cream, fruit mousses and golden rum-cakes.

We were both uncommonly captivated by this model of order, of good housekeeping, of satisfied well-being.

Now our trousers were pressed and creased; our collars, kerchiefs and shirts strikingly white.

Esenin daydreamed:

'Just wait, Anatoly, we'll even have our own press, and a car neighing at the entrance.'

Three days in a row we had Pyotr Oreshin over for dinner.

On the fourth day Esenin declared:

'He comes by not to see us, but for our meat, and to gobble up our hazel-grouse.'

Emilia was told to 'cook up a potato dinner.'

'Now, after the potatoes, we'll see how often he comes by.'

As if in fulfillment of Esenin's prophecy, after the potato dinner Oreshin disappeared for a couple of weeks.

In the evenings we'd often visit Sergei Konyonkov at his place in Presnya Street. It was a small, decrepit, white house with a studio and a tiny kitchen. Konyonkov lived in the kitchen. In that same kitchen Grigory (Konyonkov's yardkeeper, nanny and true friend) would instruct us in wisdom. Grigory had the forehead of Socrates.

Konyonkov jabbed his finger at us:

'You heed his word and put it in your memory. He speaks wisely: who are you? You are chelovek (man). And chelovek is the chelo veka (forehead of the age). Got it?'

Taking up his accordion, Konyonkov drawled out Esenin's ditties:

Ach, little apple
Ripe and ringing.
We drink vodka,
At Konyonkov's.

36

A man dropped into our bookshop on Nikitskaya and offered us a silver beaver hat at a good price. Esenin pulled the hat on top of his golden crown and walked over to the mirror. He took his time pressing a furrow on its top, bobbing it slightly, pulling his golden locks out from under the fur and fluffing them up. Pouting pretentiously, he kept looking at himself in the mirror until a smile stared back at him announcing, through his self-importance, 'Yes indeed, I really am this handsome in beaver.'

Then I tried it on.

Esenin looked on with horror at the shining black oil of my widening pupils.

'You know, Anatoly, it doesn't suit you... Not really...'

'Well, you know, Seryozha, with this hat on you look like a mushroom, a brown mushroom. It doesn't suit you either.'

'Really?'

We both sighed, deeply and mournfully. The man who had brought the hat was shifting from one foot to the other.

I said:

'Who cares if it doesn't look good on me ... It'll keep me warm, anyway ... I'd like to take it.'

Esenin smoothed the beaver's silver needles.

'It'd keep me warm too!' he uttered, dreamily.

Kozhebatkin suggested:

'You could draw lots, gentlemen.'

He laughed through nostrils bristling with hair, thick and black like watercolor brushes.

Esenin and I were indescribably overjoyed.

'Tie a knot in your handkerchief.'

Kozhebatkin produced a gray handkerchief from his pocket.

My heart missed a beat. Esenin slapped his palms against his sides in excitement, like a chicken flapping its wings.

'Well!'

Kozhebatkin extended a fist from which two little rabbit ears (the corners of the handkerchief) protruded.

Esenin took them in with his eyes, wrinkled and wiped his forehead, moved his lips, weighing something, pondering it. At last he confidently seized the end that was lumpier and more crumpled.

The customers in the shop and the hat seller crowded round.

I wound up with both the knot and the beaver hat.

From then on, the drawing of lots took firm root in our lives.

1921 pampered us with two rooms: one was not as good, the wallpaper was more faded and the furniture older, while the other one had a ministerial writing desk, English armchairs and thirty-inch borders in brown chrysanthemums on the walls.

Before me were Esenin's two fists; one of them clutched a note.

Empty hand means empty fate.

In unswerving devotion to chance, we got to the point where, standing by the door of the WC (when both of us had the urge at the same time), we'd break a matchstick in two. The lucky one, the one who drew the little head of sulphur, triumphantly proceeded to the throne-room.

37

When in February 1917 General Ivanov received the Tsar's orders to come with his St George Battalion and restore order in mutinous Petrograd, he immediately thought of his good friends in the capital and asked his adjutant in Mogilyov to buy ten dozen freshly-laid hen's eggs and a half-pood of butter.

Petrograd: former name (1914-24) of St Petersburg.

A trifling affair! His St George Battalion would march dashingly along Nevsky Propect's wood-block pavement, to the sound of the oohs and ahs of brass trumpets — and so much for the Revolution.

And while in town, the general would deliver the eggs to his good friends, warm his old legs with red side stripes before a fireplace, have a grumble, just keep creaking along, tickle himself with the new medals and the Tsar's gratitude, and back to the front he'd go.

But the eggs never reached their destination.

March.

Russia developed a schoolgirl crush on Alexander Fyodorovich Kerensky.

Alexander Kerensky (1881-1970), Prime Minister of the second Provisional Government (21 July-12 September 1917). Fled to France in 1918; moved to the USA in 1940.

Ah, these schoolgirl crushes!

Ah, a schoolgirl's fickle little heart!

The spring honeymoon was over.

June.

The Galician fields broke into blossoms of blood.

Things at the front took a turn for the worse.

August.

Kornilov pulls his non-Russian corps from the front: the Ossetian and Daghestani regiments. Generals Krymov and Krasnov assume command. Prince Gagarin with his Circassians and Ingushes is approaching Petrograd.

But Kerensky's telegrams cause the brave generals one defeat after another.

Early October.

The Cossack lieutenant Kartashov reports to General Krasnov. Kerensky comes in. He extends his hand to the officer. The other man stands at attention, stock-still, and doesn't offer his hand.

Kerensky pales:

'Lieutenant, I offered you my hand.'

'My fault, supreme commander, sir,' answers the lieutenant. 'I can't offer you mine. I am a Kornilovite.'

The officer corps was not exactly thrilled with Kerensky.

What about the workers and soldiers?

Even less so.

They let him know this in their own good time. Though not as ceremoniously as lieutenant Kartashov had.

One unlikelihood follows another, each more magnificent than the last.

1919 and 1920. The Civil War.

In 1918 Muravyov had reported to the Odessa Soviet of Deputies:

'In one day we rebuilt the 300-foot bridge demolished by the Rada and stormed Kiev. I ordered the artillery to fire on the biggest palaces, on the ten-story Grushevsky house. It burned down to ashes. I set fire to the city. I hit the palaces, the churches, the priests, the monks. On January 25 the Duma called for a truce. In answer, I ordered an asphyxiating chemical gas strike. Speaking by direct wire with Lenin, I told him that I

Mikhail Muravyov (1880-1918) Left-wing Socialist-Revolutionary, commanded a Red Army detachment. Died resisting arrest as a leader of the S-R uprising against the Bolsheviks in Simbirsk.

The Rada: the nationalist Ukrainian Parliament, established in Kiev just after the February 1917 Revolution.

wanted to go and conquer the whole world with my revolutionary forces.'

A Shakespearean monologue.

They're always trying to get literature to gaze, at least with one eye, upon life. Well, we gazed.

Once it seemed to the Imagists that a reaction against formalism was rearing its head in the arts.

The Imagist 'Supreme Soviet' (Esenin, Shershenevich, Kusikov and I) resolved at a secret session to declare a 'general mobilization' in defense of Left art.

We printed the 'order' at a small, secret press. We went out in the night to paste it up on the fences, walls and pillars of Moscow right next to the mobilization announcements of the Military Commissariat in the days of the most decisive battles with the White armies.

Early-rising cooks spread the dreadful news about 'the general mobilization order' from home to home. Crowds of terror-stricken Muscovites stood before the 'order.' Some understood nothing at all, others read only the headlines; they grabbed hold of their heads and hurried off. 'The order' was compelling 'all! all! all!' to gather on such and such a date on Theater Square with banners and slogans demanding the preservation of Left art. Then there would be a procession to the Moscow Soviet, speeches and a presentation of 'claims.'

Theatre Square is located in front of the Bolshoi.

Around noon Shershenevich and Kusikov ran into our bookshop on Nikitskaya.

Their eyes were wide with fear and their faces white. Kusikov, slowly moving his numb tongue, asked:

'Y-you're ... still ... in business?'

Esenin looked alarmed:

'And you?'

'We've ... already been...'

'Already been what?'

'Closed... because of the "mobilization" ... and...'

With cold fingers Kusikov pulled the narrow 'notification' slip out of his pocket and showed it to us.

Esenin inspected the dread seal.

'Tolya, let's go ... for a walk...'

He reached for his hat.

Just then a black automobile stopped in front of the store's plate glass window. Two men in leather jackets stepped out of it.

Esenin set the hat aside. His salvation 'walk' had occurred to him too late. The men in black leather entered the shop. Within minutes Esenin, Shershenevich, Kusikov and I were at the Moscow Cheka.

The Cheka (1917-22), special commission charged with prevention of counter-revolutionary activities.

The investigator, making an effort to swallow a chuckle, began the interrogation.

Esenin said:

'But dear sir, I'm with the Bolsheviks ... I'm truly with the October Revolution ... Have you read my poem:

My land is my mother,
And I am a Bolshevik.

And this fellow (he pointed at me) wrote about you... He exalted the Red terror:

In this heap of skulls
Lies our Red vengeance...

Shershenevich gently touched Esenin's shoulder:

'Wait a second, Seryozha, wait a second... Comrade investigator, unfortunately, Russian literature of late has begun to smell of Buninism and Merezhkovskyism.'

Ivan Bunin (1870-1955), Russian writer, Nobel Prize winner. Emigrated to France in 1918.

Merezhkovsky, see p.20

'Dear sir, he's telling the truth... It's been stinking... It's started to reek...'

Stern and angry letters crept out of the investigator's gold fountain pen, but the finger with which he scratched his crown, ruffling its tow-haired down, was — unforgivably for such an institution — good-natured and not serious enough.

'Sign here.'

We silently inscribed our names.

In an hour we were celebrating, treating Shershenevich and Kusikov to young Kakhetian wine at our place on Bogoslovsky.

The next day, in accordance with the investigator's instructions, we showed up on Theater Square to call off the mobilization.

Some black-haired girls didn't want to disperse; they demanded 'poems,' while a curly-headed youth wanted 'speeches.'

We cryptically threw up our hands. A detachment of ten horsemen from the mounted militia filled us with pride.

Esenin whispered in my ear:

'We're like Marat ... When he wrote about this minister, Jacques Necker, they sent twelve thousand cavalrymen against him.'

38

How-Much-fer-Salt was leaving for the Crimea.

Our affairs were in such a state that it was vital that one of us remain in Moscow. We drew lots. The trip fell to me. We agreed that Esenin would get the next leave of absence.

When I returned a month later, Esenin read me the first chapter of *Pugachev*.

Pugachev, a narrative poem about the peasant rebellion led by Yemelyan Pugachev at the time of Catharine the Great. (18th C.).

Oh, how tired I am and my leg ails me so,
The road neighs into the frightening distance...

From the first lines I felt flesh and blood in the language. Its heels and soles pressed into the earth, the verse stands firm.

I'd brought back the first act of *The Fools' Plot*.

We set out for a drink to celebrate my return and the beginnings of our dramatic poems. How-Much-fer-Salt joined us.

On Nikitsky Boulevard, in a red stone house, on the seventh floor, at Zoya Petrovna Shatova's place, you could get not only tsarist-times 'white-capped' vodka, all sorts of 'Pertsovka' (pepper brandy) and Smirnoff's 'Zubrovka' (sweet-grass vodka), but old Burgundy and black English rum as well.

Zoya Shatova's 'salon for intimate meetings' was well known in the bohemian as well as crime world. Her 'salon' is also described in Bulgakov's play *Zoika's Apartment*.

We gaily ran up the unending stairs. We rang the doorbell three times according to the secret code. The door yawned open. Esenin recoiled.

'Please! Please! Come in. Come in. And you ... and you...' a man with a revolver said, very politely. 'And now, your papers, please!'

We'd been quite lucky of late, chancing upon these 'pleasant' meetings.

Red Army soldiers armed with rifles sat in the corridor while policemen searched the apartment.

'I am the poet Esenin!'

'I am the poet Mariengof!'

'Very nice to meet you.'

'Please let us go...'

'So sorry...'

There was nothing for it — we stayed...

'Will you let us have supper?'

'Please be so kind. You'll even find some libations here. Isn't that true, Zoya Petrovna?'

Zoya Petrovna tried to draw out her lips into an obsequious smile, but they only made a pathetic, frightened grimace.

How-Much-fer-Salt's cheekbones were twitching, he was picking at a wart and unfolding his credentials one after another, each about the size of a linen pillow case.

Zoya Petrovna's guests, sitting frozen in armchairs, on sofas, on chairs, had lost both their appetite and their loquacity.

Lubyanka: a square in the center of Moscow, the location of Cheka headquarters and prison.

At one in the morning, in the company of some sixty people, we set out for Lubyanka in two freight trucks.

Esenin had methodically and sternly equipped himself, me and How-Much-fer-Salt with Zoya Petrovna's pillows, blankets, heads of cheese, goose, chicken, pork brisket and a leg of veal.

In the lock-up that same businesslike sense and efficiency prevailed. Our bunks, covered with velvety blankets, looked very cozy.

Suddenly a pillow vanished.

Esenin barked to the whole cell:

'If that pillow isn't on my bunk in ten minutes, I'll call for a general search... You hear me... You... citizens... Go to hell!'

Somehow the pillow resurfaced.

The order for our release was signed after three days.

39

Esenin left with How-Much-fer-Salt for Bukhara. Another comic figure had been added to our friend's staff, an engineer named Lev.

Lev stumped around on short, crooked legs, his crown topped by a large bald patch — pink as a young girl's heel. His eyes were sad and all of him was sad, like a chemist's phial.

Lev loved to talk about spicy, fatty and rich dishes, though he himself had gastritis and ate only kasha, which he'd cook in his own little copper saucepan, on his own small primus stove.

From Minsk to Chita, from Batumi all the way to Samarkand, there was no place where he wouldn't find some relative of his.

That's how he won over How-Much-fer-Salt's heart.

Esenin would say:

'What a great chap! You'll never be lost with him; on the verge of being impaled by a Turk, he'll run into some sixth cousin once-removed.'

Before their departure, How-Much-fer-Salt set down these conditions for Lev:

'You want to join my crew an' go to Turkestan, buy yerself an engineer's cap. Without a velvet cap-band, what fool's gonna believe you finished a polytechnic?'

Lev was stingy to the point of naivete, and the prospect of such an expense cast him into an abyss of dejection.

Esenin tried to persuade How-Much-fer-Salt:

'All the same nobody'll believe it.'

Lev grumbled:

'Pesteging me about that cap, like a laugel leaf stuck to my ass.'

'Not a laurel leaf, Lev, but a bathhouse leaf,' Esenin corrected him with the proper Russian saying. 'A bathhouse leaf is birch...'

Literally: 'to stick like a bathhouse leaf', Russian proverb meaning 'to stick like a leech.' In Russian steam baths people beat themselves with birch twigs.

'Same thing. I'm saying to this fool: you want a silly cap hege, while over thege I could buy thgee poods of floug for that money.'

How-Much-fer-Salt became angry:

'You don't understand! I need an engineer that'll look nice. So he can be looking out the carriage window...'

'Then why don't you put an engineer's cap on the train guard?'

How-Much-fer-Salt's cheekbones were twitching.

Lev waved his hand hopelessly:

'To gell with you... I'll go to the Sukhagevka market tomoggow.'

The money we'd scraped together for Esenin's trip was a little on the low side. We asked Lev for advice on how we might increase our capital.

Making sure How-Much-fer-Salt didn't hear him,

Lev told us that in Bukhara gold 10-ruble coins went for three times the Moscow rate.

Esenin gave him some money:

'Buy me some.'

The next day instead of ten-ruble coins Lev brought us a heap of wedding rings.

We burst out laughing.

The rings were ridiculous, enormous — you could run a napkin through them.

Lev reassured us:

'You don't need to get married, Segyozha; you're going to sell them. I'm telling you you'll make money hand oveg fist.'

When he came back, Esenin drolly recounted how Lev had run all around Tashkent with the rings, darting in and out of bazaars and shops, and how in the end he'd had to let them go at a loss.

Lev was depressed for a week and kept muttering to himself with cold lips, as if casting some spell:

'Losses! What losses...'

I received a letter from Esenin:

Dearest Tolya, greetings and kisses to you.

Right now I'm sitting in the train carriage. For exactly three days I've been looking out the window at this damned Samara, and I'm not at all sure whether I'm really experiencing all this or reading *Dead Souls* and *The Inspector General*. How-Much-fer-Salt is drunk, assuring some friend of his he's written *Yuri Miloslavsky*, that the political big shots are all his friends, that he's got 'lots of couriers, couriers, and more couriers.' Lev is

A reference to the braggart Khlestakov from Gogol's *Inspector General.*

sulking and always asking me if I wouldn't like to be eating a bowl of Ukrainian borscht right now.

I remember your sour face that time you were talking about herring. If you want to know what I look like, eat a piece and look at yourself in the mirror.

All the same I'm having a fine time on this trip, really — I'm even glad that I gave goddamn Moscow the old slip. Right now I'm collecting myself and looking inward. Our last binge really flummoxed me. I will absolutely not drink like that anymore, and today, as a matter of fact, I begged off altogether, so I could watch How-Much-fer-Salt get sloshed. My God, what filth — and I was probably in even worse shape.

For some reason the weather is colder here this year than at home. In some places there's even snow. So I don't go round with nothing on and I sleep under my coat. Of course, our stock of foodstuffs is so low that I keep asking Lev in my turn, as a reflex, 'Wouldn't you like to be eating a sausage right now, Lev?' Yes, one day, two days, three, four, five, six days, we've been going and going, but you look out the window and still you see this damn Samara, like some enchanted place.

The carriage is nice, of course, but nonetheless it's too bad I can't stand still. All this shaking makes it hard for my turbulent mind to think straight. A horse (not a foal) ran after our train again, but now I'm in the habit of saying, 'Nature, you're imitating Esenin.'

In short, my friend, I often think of you and our dear Emilia and always we come back to the same old question: 'What do you think Anatoly's eating these days, Lev?'

All in all the trip's been splendid. I've always told myself, in fact, that there's no harm in an outing, especially when the butter is 16-17 roubles in Moscow, and here it's in the 25-to-30 range.

On the one hand, it's economical, and on the other hand (I can hear Lev in the next compartment telling How-Much-fer-Salt what he thinks of his mother), this 'other hand' is our next dish.

You see, all this is rather amusing and diverting, so I have no problem finishing this letter now, the sooner to part with it. Oh, I wasn't wrong when I told myself traveling with 'How-Much-fer-Salt' would be a lot of fun.

Greetings to Konyonkov, Sergei and David Samoilovich.

Your Sergei.

Sergei Bystrov and David Samoilovich Eisenstadt (see p. 74) — partners at the bookshop.

PS. It's been four days since I wrote you this letter, and we're still in Samara. Today I stepped out onto the platform, full of yearning (that is, joy), walked up to the newspapers posted on the wall, and got an eyeful of the Samara Writers' Union savaging the Imagists. I had no idea we were so popular here.

40

During Esenin's absence, I met the Kamerny Theater actress Anna Nikritina (my future wife) in Shershenevich's bookshop.

Once, on a mild April night, we were sitting by the Stone Bridge. The reflected dome of the Cathedral of Christ the Savior floated along the dark water of the Moskva River like a huge golden boat. The occasional automobile, its headlights goggling and wheels shhhhhing, rushed past. The waves beat their chill glassy body against the stone.

I yearned to speak of the extraordinary, with extraordinary words.

I picked up a rock and hurled it into the river at the dome's reflection.

The golden boat exploded in sparks, spangling splinters and black cracks.

'Look!'

The sturdy, smooth golden vessel floated anew on the river's surface. There was not a memory, no trace of the cobblestone that had just cleft it.

I spoke of friendship, likening it to the cathedral's reflection in the river, and of the women we'd had, who were like the rock.

Then I tied a knot in my handkerchief, dipped one end in the water, tightened the wet cloth some more and, handing it to Anna, said:

'Now try to untie it.'

She raised her eyes to me.

'What for?'

'The knot's hard as rock. This is just what my friendship with Esenin is like.'

I told her of our years of shared happiness and sorrow, our hopes and disillusions.

She smiled:

'You might have better luck with iambic rhymes.'

It struck me as a little silly, and I felt rather embarrassed at these words parading like self-important turkey cocks.

I parted with Esenin some years later. But today I know that the split happened not in 1924, after his return from abroad, but much, much earlier. Maybe even in Shershenevich's bookshop, when I caught my first glimpse of Anna. Or maybe it was that night, when I yearned to describe our friendship with extraordinary words.

41

Clouds of silver dust rose from the roadways. A hoary, feeble yardkeeper, not unlike Konyonkov's wooden statue of 'Old Fogie,' was moving about Bogoslovsky Lane. He seemed to be walking not on legs, but on low-cut stumps of thick birch. The yardkeeper held a small, green watering can. With it he doused the dust-emitting cobblestones. He moved slowly, inclining just as slowly the watering can's thin neck, which reluctantly snorted out bright, wee splashes onto the hot stone.

Once the 'old fogie' had been a gardener, he had watered tender pink gilly-flowers with his little green watering can. He was useful then, as were his little watering can and flowers that smelled of good French soap. But now the moistened cobblestones were starting to emit dust again before he had even reached the end of his sidewalk, less than twenty-five yards long.

Anna and I were coming back from the horse races.

A trotter's horseshoes were beating on the pavement as if upon piano keys.

Anna hadn't once been to our place. I spent a long time cajoling, pleading, tempting her with the prospect of Emilia's rare culinary skill.

When she finally consented, I ran up three flights of stairs without stopping and pressed the doorbell, forgetting to draw my finger back. The crazed bell bawled and bawled, loud as my heart.

When the door burst open and I saw Emilia's astonished, afrighted and questioning eyes, I instantly invented a defense against them in the form of a transparent lie:

'I'm dying of hunger! Food! Food! F...!'

Sacks of flour, dried apricots, rice and raisins slouched in the corridor.

I flew into the room. Suitcases, baskets, bags.

'Sergei Alexandrovich has arrived. He ran out to look for you.'

I started jumping up and down like a child, like a child I clapped my hands, like a child I seized Anna's hands, whose warmth was gradually ebbing.

The sun, unusually hot for spring, was beating at the window.

'I had better go...'

She freed her hands — now two small, hostile pieces of ice — from my grasp. I took her home. As we said goodbye, I tried to catch her eye and couldn't — her brows knitted and her lashes trailed down her cheeks, like those long, old-fashioned skirts.

I found Esenin at Pegasus' Stall.

For some reason, embracing him, I too hid my eyes.

That evening How-Much-fer-Salt lamented:

'I'll never, I give you my word, I'll never in my life ever go anywhere with Sergei again. He crammed the whole carriage with flour and raisins. At night, the scoundrel, he'd arrange to have it loaded. I'm supposed to be the terror down there, representing the central authority, fully empowered. And there he is, swiping raisins from the bazaar and stuffing them in the carriage. I allowed him and Lev two poods each, but those cretins, they crammed in six poods apiece.'

Esenin in my ear:

'Twelve!'

'Strutting his stuff in front of them minor local poets, tossing money around, and running a supermarket right out of the central authority's rail carriage. Knocking himself out haggling with those raisin merchants! And me, what kind of ... "central authority" am I after that?'

'So what if we got those dried apricots and raisins! What about me writing the fourth and fifth chapters of *Pugachev* in your carriage? What about that? I'm immortalizing you, you son of a bitch, I'm giving you eternity. And all you can think of is those dried apricots!'

At the mention of 'eternity,' How-Much-fer-Salt's words died on his lips, and he began radiating tenderness, warmth and peace like some little window under a muslin curtain in a slushy, god-forsaken Penza alley, a window lit up by a kerosene lamp with a pink glass shade.

42

Anna was leaving for Kiev. Due to some tender inhibition, as well as some comical embarrassment, I decided not to accompany her to the railway station.

She lived in Gazetny Lane. The route to Alexander Station ran along Nikitskaya Street, right past our bookshop.

Alexander Station: former name of Kiev Station.

The train was due to depart at about three. Worried I'd be late, I started getting ready to go down to the shop at 10:30. Normally, we never turned up before two. And in the summer of his *Pugachev* and my *Fool's Plot*, we'd drop in for perhaps an hour after lunch, and even that not every day.

Esenin was surprised:

'Are you crazy? At this ungodly hour...'

'Today's usually busy.'

Fixing me with his gaze, he asked snidely:

'Have some business, hm? Well, go on, go on, take care of business.'

He went with me, to bear witness.

When we arrived, I sat by the window, my fidgeting eyes catching furtive glances beyond the glass.

Whenever a customer came in, Esenin would elbow me:

'Go on! Take care of business...'

I gave him a pleading look.

But he only replied:

'Anatoly Borisovich, would you mind getting Sheller-Mikhailov down from the top shelf.'

As if on purpose to annoy me, that hack had written some fifty volumes. I grinned at both the customer and Esenin. And at the latter's obnoxious manner of addressing me formally by my name and patronymic. I stammered:

'Comrade Esenin...'

And then from my perch atop the stepladder, balancing a three-and-a-half-foot-tall stack of books in my hands, I caught sight through the window, through a silver spume of dust, of a cabman with the familiar little basket at his feet.

It's hard to keep your balance in a situation like that. On the cab seat I glimpsed the cambric blouse with a small tie and brown skirt. As if she weren't an actress in a theatre famous for its aesthetic productions of Hoffmann, Claudel and Wilde, but a schoolgirl in the sixth form, going on vacation to provincial Mirgorod.

So it wasn't my fault, but fate's — it was punishment for Esenin being so implacable and hard-hearted.

The entire three-and-a-half-foot mountain of Sheller-Mikhailov crashed down, its tough *Niva* bindings clattering onto Esenin's head.

As for me, I flew out of the shop like a cork from a siphon, forever exposing my heart to the nastiest shafts and most virulent taunts.

43

We stayed in Moscow for the summer. Esenin worked on *Pugachev*, I on *The Fools' Plot.* For the sake of peace and quiet, we'd close our doors to both our friends and Esenin's girlfriends until lunch. We even put out a sign to this effect at the entrance.

Those who ignored our decree had to deal with Emilia. Short of biting them in the haunches, she was an excellent Cerberus.

Whereas I derived the material for my historical poems from two or three old books, Esenin's source was the academic edition of Pushkin's collected works.

Esenin had not read anything besides Pushkin's *History of Pugachev's Rebellion* and *The Captain's*

Daughter, and when his conscience began to gnaw at him, he'd rationalize that in any case Pokrovsky could never write better than Pushkin.

Mikhail Pokrovsky (1868-1932) historian, director of the Communist Academy and the Red Professor Institute. Author of the 5-volume *History of Russia.*

I love his *Pugachev.* Esenin contrived to write with a lyricist's marvelous naivete about stern characters and themes that were not lyrical at all.

Esenin's poem is like those old orthodox icons in which the icon-painters portrayed God resting, after the creation of the world, on a sleeping-bench beneath a patchwork quilt. On the floor they painted his freshly-doffed felt boots. God himself was a ginger-bearded Novgorodian muzhik with yellow, calloused heels.

Peter the Great had such icons burned as offensive to the faith. But Roman popes and cardinals had a better eye for art. The icons in Italian cathedrals feature the saints sporting the popular fashions of the Renaissance.

We read *Pugachev* and *The Fools' Plot* to friends, a chapter at a time.

Once we had Konyonkov, Meyerhold, Gustav Shpet, and Yakulov for a reading. When we finished, Meyerhold started talking about staging productions of the two poems at his theater.

'We'll invite Konyonkov to design the sets. He'll make us those huge wooden idols of his.'

Konyonkov's eyes narrowed:

'What!?'

'I said that you could make us those wooden idols...'

'Wooden idols?'

Konyonkov banged his glass on the table so hard that tiny fragments of it scattered everywhere.

'I mean your statues ... of wood...'

'For this low farce of yours?'

Konyonkov stood up:

'Well, forgive me, Seryozha. Forgive me, Anatoly. I'll go ... Away from the wooden idols...'

He was extremely offended.

Meyerhold couldn't understand how Konyonkov had been insulted or what all the fuss was about.

'How can you be so insensitive, Vsevolod! Wooden idols! How can you say that? You don't stroke a woman on her paunch as gently as he caresses his "marsh muzhiks" and "old fogies"... He never unveils them in his studio in front of strangers. All the doors must be locked before he divests them of their canvas covers, as if he were disrobing his bride on their wedding night... And you with your "wooden idols". How can you say that.'

Esenin sermonized, while Yakulov comforted Meyerhold in his own inimitable manner:

'He's ... g-he, g-he ... Asia, Vsevolod, Asia ... He's sculpted the Greek queen ... He came from Athens in a tuxedo ... Out of his spade-like beard he fashioned a little goatee. Well, a European artist, I thought. And once ... g-he, g-he ... he came by to my place ... There was champagne, fruit, beautiful women ... g-he, g-he ... He says, "Let's go to my place, to Presnya, it's, g-he, g-he, dull here." I wondered what surprising things he'd have to show me after that "Greek archipelago" trip. He brought me into his kitchen, put two bottles of vodka ... g-he, g-he ... some pickled cucumbers, onions... He sat on the stove bench, produced his accordion ... took off his shoes, and then ... g-he, g-he ... he started to warble:

"We sowed and sowed the millet." And made me sing, too ... Just fancy, beautiful women, ... g-he, g-he ... a white waistcoat ... A European artist ... g-he, g-he ... Just Asia, Vsevolod, Asia.'

44

More than anything in the world Esenin dreaded syphilis. A pimple the size of a bread crumb would bud on his nose, and he would go from mirror to mirror, gloomy and sullen.

He'd ask fifty times a day:

'Syphilis. It might be, right? Right?'

Once he even went down to Rumyantsev Library to read up on the symptoms of this terrible malady.

Rumyantsev Libaray was renamed Lenin Library in 1925. The biggest library in Russia.

After that it got even worse. At the slightest sign:

'*Lues Venerea*!'

When he arrived back from Turkestan with How-Much-fer-Salt, his gums started to bleed slightly as a result of his having been constantly munching on dried apricots.

In front of anyone and everyone he'd pull up his lip:

'Look, it's bleeding ... isn't it? First stage, right? Right?'

Once Kusikov was having a party. Esenin sat next to Meyerhold, who told him:

'You know, Seryozha, I really am in love with your wife ... with Zinaida Nikolayevna. You won't be angry with me if we get married?'

Esenin jokingly bowed down before Meyerhold:

'Take her, do me the favor. I'll be grateful to you to my dying day.'

As soon as they left the table, he yanked up his lip for Meyerhold:

'Look ... The gum ... there...'

Meyerhold uttered meaningfully:

'Yesss...'

All the color went out of Esenin's face, like a cotton print faded by the July sun.

Later he took aside How-Much-fer-Salt and discreetly informed him, in a tragic whisper:

'I've got syphilis. Vsevolod said so. And you an' I were drinking from the same glass. That means...'

How-Much-fer-Salt's knees gave way.

Esenin led him to a couch, sat him down and poured him a glass of water:

'Drink it!'

How-Much-fer-Salt gulped it down. But his cheekbones kept right on jumping.

'Maybe I should splash you?' Esenin asked. And he splashed him.

How-Much-fer-Salt stared into nothingness with unseeing eyes.

Esenin sat down next to him. His head, like the wooden ball from a ball-and-cup toy, fell from his shoulders into his hands.

They sat like that for some ten minutes. Then they got up and, dragging their feet along the parquet floor, went out into the hall.

Kusikov and I caught up with them at the door.

'Where you off to?'

'We're going home. We've got syphilis.'

And they left.

At six o'clock the next morning, Esenin roused How-Much-fer-Salt:

'Get up... We're going to the doctor.'

How-Much-fer-Salt instantly sat up in bed and started jamming both feet into one underpants' leg.

I tried to make light of it:

'Misha, your palsy of the brain's already set in!'

But when he darted a tortured glance at me, I bitterly regretted my joke.

His pupils were wide with horror, like drops of ink fallen on blotting paper.

The poor devil believed me.

Esenin knotted his tie with a forced calm and cold fingers.

Then How-Much-fer-Salt, forgetting to put on his jodhpurs, began pulling on his high boots right over his underpants.

I put a hand on his shoulder:

'Even if you are a "full general" now, Misha, all the same you're not entitled to a senator's uniform yet.'

'And you just keep on cracking jokes!' said Esenin without turning round, his shoulders quivering. 'Even with the stink of Browning bullets in the air. And you call yourself a friend...'

By 7:30 they were yanking the bellpull at a heavy oaken door with a polished brass name-plate.

The housemaid, who had not yet had time to conceal her early-morning dreams and her voluptuous body behind a starched apron, gave off a warm breath, like mist from a morning marsh stream. She opened the chained door just a crack and muttered something about the early hour and the professor's old bones needing their rest.

Esenin hammered on the door with his fists until he heard an answering cough, hoarse rasps and 'Ohs!' from the far room.

The old bones rose up from their bed to prescribe, for one patient, a dental elixir and soft toothbrush, and for the other:

'Bromide, my good man, bromide is all you need.'

In parting, the professor wheezed:

'I've been in practice for forty-five years, my good man, but never has anyone gone so far as to try and break my door down... No, my good man... It would be a different matter if you had come with a real problem. But this... What are you, Bolsheviks? Tut-tut! Well, keep well, old chaps.'

45

The Hermitage. A merry, calico crowd seated on benches. Signor Vesuvio and Don Madrido — clowns from abroad — on the open stage. The signor's nose is like a Vologda turnip, the Don's like a Poltava cucumber. Don Madrido performs somersaults on a colorful Russian carpet. Signor catches him by his wide pants.

The Hermitage park reeks of ripe mushrooms. Esenin once found two wild strawberries near the iron fence.

I haven't been to Leningrad in a long while. I wonder if that sweet, ridiculous little grass still winds its way between the slabs of Nevsky's wood-block pavement, as it did in those wondrous days.

The Hermitage is the world-famous architectural ensemble in St Petersburg housing the Hermitage Museum of World Art. Built by Catherine the Great in 1764, it also includes the Winter Palace (the royal residence until 1917), the Hermitage Theatre and the park.

Signor Vesuvio and Don Madrido are replaced by a famous Russian ballerina.

We gaze at her young, supple calves. Her toe, like a spear, is thrust into the plank platform. But her cheeks sag, and there's a 50-year-old puffiness beneath her eyes. Art is a miraculous thing.

On a decrepit, disinterested piano, a man with dark, tired eyelids bangs out 'Swan Lake.'

George Yakulov comes over to us. He is wearing a violet service jacket made of old drapery and tapping his yellow leggings with a thin walking stick. A fashionable fellow. With this very stick, in white gloves, he had led his company into battle against the Germans. Later he was all ajingle with St. George's crosses on orange ribbons.

Isadora Duncan (1878-1927) the American dancer whose expressive, free style of dance (barefoot, in a loose tunic) was inspired by the figures on ancient Greek vases. She toured extensively and founded schools of modern dance in London, Paris, Berlin and Moscow.

Yakulov looks at us, enigmatically screwing up one olive-like eye while the other sparkles as if generously drenched in olive oil.

'Would you like me to introduce you to Isadora Duncan?'

Esenin jumped up:

'Where is she? Where?'

'Here ... g-he, g-he ... An ama-azing woman...'

Esenin grabbed Yakulov by the sleeve:

'Lead the way!'

We rushed off to the Mirror Hall and then the Winter Hall, from the Winter Hall to the Summer Hall, from the Summer Hall to the operetta, from the operetta back to the park scanning intently the benches.

No Isadora Duncan in sight.

'Damn ... g-he, g-he ... Nope ... She's gone ... Damn.'

And once more from the Mirror Hall to the Winter Hall, from the Winter Hall to the operetta, to the Summer Hall, to the park.

'George, my dear man, she's here, here.'

'Why don't you sniff her out, Seryozha,' I said.

'I will. And you just keep writing two love letters a day to Kiev and shut your trap.'

So I had to shut my trap.

Isadora Duncan didn't turn up. Esenin grew sombre and vexed.

Now something seems fateful about the burning and inexplicable desire he felt that day to meet a woman he'd never seen before, a woman who was destined to play such a huge, grievous and — I would even say — ruinous role in his life.

But don't misunderstand me: Duncan's ruinous effect on Esenin in no way diminishes this remarkable woman, this marvelous person and artist of genius.

46

How-Much-fer-Salt fell in love. He took to shaving, changing his motley embroidered Turkish skullcaps, polishing his boots with American wax and powdering his nose. He had half a dozen shirts made out of white Bokhara silk.

To be perfectly honest, I was responsible for this tragedy. After all, I knew that How-Much-fer-Salt loved good things.

And the woman to whom I introduced him was the very definition of a Good Thing. You could have furnished your apartment with her.

Our friend had no apartment, but he did have the train carriage. It was because of that carriage that he'd had Lev decked out with an 'engineer's' cap. It would be awful if he were to take the Thing as his wife and decorate his carriage with her presence.

I told him, from the bottom of my heart:

'It'd be better if I gave you a carpet!'

That only made him mad.

In the evenings Esenin and I would worry about our friend's future. Esenin would say, as in the old days:

'The guy's wasting away. Makes you want to cry-y...'

47

Anna was back.

Cold autumn nights and a moon like the yolk of a hard-boiled egg.

I'd been waiting on a little bench on Tverskoi Boulevard, opposite the Kamerny Theater, since eleven o'clock.. As a friend of Meyerhold's and thus a foe of Tairov I was banned from the theater. How long ago that all seems now. Today when I run into Meyerhold I barely touch my hat, while Tairov and I are a bit more than just friends.

Sometimes the rehearsals would go until one, two, or even three in the morning.

When I got home, Esenin and How-Much-fer-Salt would make fun of me. They promised to give me a warm top hat with earmuffs. They called me 'Brambill' (*Princess Brambilla* was playing at the Kamerny). They called Anna 'little monkey' or 'marmoset.'

Esenin came up with some ditties.

Here I think Anna quite lovely, and he sings:

Ach, the dear marmoset-soul
Not too easy on the eyes.

And when she's over at our place, Esenin sings the exact same ditty with a slight alteration:

Ach, the dear marmoset-soul
Sure is easy on the eyes.

At night I'd hear troubled whispers on the other side of the wall: How-Much-fer-Salt and Esenin worrying about my future.

48

Yakulov was having a party in his studio. Some time after midnight, Duncan came by.

A red tunic flowing in light folds; red hair with a shimmer of copper; a large body, stepping lightly and easily.

Her eyes, like saucers of blue faience, scanned the room and froze on Esenin.

The small, tender mouth smiled at him.

Isadora was lying on a couch with Esenin at her feet.

She dipped her hand in his curls and said in broken Russian:

'Golden head.'

It was astounding that she, who knew no more than ten Russian words, knew these two.

Later she kissed him on the lips.

Then her mouth, small and red as a bullet wound, pleasantly mangled the Russian sounds:

'Angel.'

She kissed him again and said:

'Damn.'

At four in the morning Isadora and Esenin left together.

How-Much-fer-Salt sat down by me and, in utmost desperation, started outlining a plan for 'our Vyatka's rescue.'

'I'll take him away.'

'He won't go.'

'To Persia.'

'If only to Persia...'

We left Yakulov's at dawn. We strolled the deserted streets with heavy hearts.

The ballerina A.M. Balashova emigrated to France after the Revolution. Her house was expropriated and in 1921 given over to Isadora Duncan for her dancing school. In Paris, oddly, Balashova rented a house in the rue de la Pompe that belonged to Duncan.

49

The next day we went over to Isadora's place.

The address was 20 Prechistenka Street, Balashova's former private residence. Heavy marble staircases, rooms in various styles: Empire, like some Moscow restaurants, favored by merchants; Mauritanian, like the Sandunov public bathhouses. The winter garden consisted of sickly cactuses and cheerless palms, as depressed and sad as the scrawny beasts in iron cages at the city zoo. The furniture was heavy and gilt. Brocade, damask, velvet.

Isadora's room contained armchairs, couches, and tables covered over in light French fabrics, Venetian kerchiefs, and motley Russian chintz. Everything that could be pressed into service to conceal bad taste and disagreeable luxury had been extracted from her many trunks.

Isadora smiled tenderly and, wrinkling her nose, said:

'*C'est Balachoff* ... bad *chambre* ... Isadora *fichu chale achetra* ... many ruska *chale* ...'

There were mattresses and pillows on the floor covered with rugs and furs.

The chandeliers were veiled in red silk. Isadora didn't like white electric light. Rumor had it that she was over fifty.

In 1921 Isadora Duncan was only 44.

On a small table by the bed stood a large portait of Gordon Craig.

Esenin took it and scrutinized it. Then he sucked in his dry, slightly chapped lips.

'Your husband?'

'*Qu'est-ce que c'est*?'

'*Mari... epoux...*'

'*Qui, mari... bi* ... Craig writes *travaillait, travaillait...* Craig *genie*.'

Esenin jabbed his own chest.

'I'm a genius, too! Esenin is a genius ... a genius! Me ... Esenin, I'm the genius, and Craig is crap!'

Grimacing contemptuously he slips Craig's portrait under a pile of sheet music and old journals.

'*Adieu!*'

Isadora, in raptures:

'*Adieu*.' She makes a slight gesture of farewell.

Esenin furrows his brow: 'Now, Isadora, dance! You understand, Isadora? Dance for us!'

He imagines he's Herod demanding a dance from Salome.

'Dance? *Bon*!'

Duncan dons Esenin's cap and jacket. The music is sensual, unfamiliar, disturbing.

Isadora is an Apache. Her scarf is the woman partner. A frightening and marvelous dance.

The scarf's narrow pink body coils and twists in her hands. She snaps its spine, her restless fingers wring its neck. The round silk head droops pitiably, tragically.

When Isadora finishes the dance, her diaphanous partner's corpse lies stretched out on the carpet in convulsions.

Esenin soon became her master, her sovereign. Like a dog, she would kiss the hand he'd just raised to strike her, and kiss the eyes in which hatred burned more often than love.

Even so, he was no more than a dancing partner, like that scrap of pink fabric — tragic and bereft of will.

She danced.

She led the dance.

50

Our friend Sasha Sakharov, an inveterate composer of ditties, was already bawling out:

Tolya walks around unwashed
But Seryozha's clean as a whistle
For Seryozha's spending nights
With Duncan on Prechistenka.

A disagreeable unrest seized our days.

A pinkish semi-twilight. Light folds of red silk flowing from Isadora's large, soft shoulders.

Esenin gives How-Much-fer-Salt a cheap little music box.

'Crank it, Misha, and I'll put myself in pretzels.'

How-Much-fer-Salt cranks the little wire handle. The box squeaks out some folk music.

Slipping off his patent-leather shoes, in bare feet on the downy French rugs, Esenin performs his 'pretzels,' staggering like a drunkard. Duncan watches him with her enamored blue faience saucers.

'*C'est la Russie ... ca c'est la Russie...*'

The glasses shake on the table, spilling warm champagne.

Esenin's yellow heels gyrate like tumbler pigeons.

'Wonderful!'

Esenin stops, big cold drops clinging to his ashen forehead. His eyes, too, are like cold drops, enraged, almost colorless.

'Isadora, cigarette!'

Duncan hands him one.

'Champagne!'

And she goes for champagne.

Esenin empties the glass in one gulp and immediately pours himself another to the rim.

Isadora wraps her tender, soft arms about his neck.

Tea, diluted with milk seems to pour into those blue faience saucers.

She whispers in her broken Russian:

'Esenin is strong ... very strong...'

This pastime took place seven nights a week, month in and month out.

Once I asked Isádora for some water. She had forgotten that there was such a thing as water.

Champagne, cognac, vodka.

At the beginning of the winter How-Much-fer-Salt had to go to the Caucasus. We started scheming to spirit Esenin out of Moscow. We finally seduced him with Persia.

As luck would have it, Esenin missed the train.

How-Much-fer-Salt sacrificed Lev in his engineer's cap. After the third bell, he kicked the poor devil off the train with instructions to find Esenin and catch up with the train in Rostov.

A week later they finally managed to get away.

I received a postcard from Rostov:

Dear Tolya,

The devil take you for getting me into this mess. In the first place, I'm staying at Nina's here in Rostov and cursing for all I'm worth. That carriage of yours is gone. Lev got us tickets but traveling in a train like this is the same as hanging impaled on some Turk's spike. As a result I've lost all faith in your resources. All of this is on account of your youth and his stupidity. Thursday I'm going to Tbilisi and I'll be glad to meet up with Misha there. It'll mean an end to all these torments.

Rostov is nothing but mud and mush, and this 'Segyozha' who haggles with everybody over two lousy kopecks. Everywhere you go with him you burn with shame. Say hello to Isadora, Irma and Ilya Ilyich. I think they've had a good airing out by now and have probably forgotten about me.

Irma — Isadora's adopted daughter; Ilya Ilyich — Isadora's secretary.

Ah, well, out of sight, out of mind. I won't shed any tears, naturally.

What a damn fool you are, redhead! And I hardly know any better, having listened to you.

Damned Persia.

Sergei.

The day after I received this missive, Esenin arrived back to Moscow in person.

51

The Thing settled in our little white carriage on the Turkestan railroad.

The Thing had an exquisite nose, soft golden tresses, lips well drawn in bright oil paint and eyes in transparent blue water-color. Her eyes were unfriendly like a room left unheated and unfit for habitation.

Along with our big Thing, a multitude of little things took up residence in our tiny carriage: teeny blue tablecloths, teensy-weensy plush carpets, itty-bitty curtains, and wee silver spoons, vases, ash-trays, and flasks.

Whenever How-Much-fer-Salt started breathing too loudly, angry folds gathered on big Thing's nose.

'Please, be more careful! You'll break my Baccarat.'

In some cases I could not contain myself from sarcastically intoning:

'The little bottles, though, aren't Baccarat, but

Brocharat.' (There was such a perfumery firm in Moscow before the Revolution.)

The Thing puckered her lips into a little tube.

'Of course, Anatoly Borisovich, you can say that if you've never seen quality glass and porcelain. After all you and Esenin even have paper linen on your beds, even our cook at home would be ashamed to sleep on such beds as that.'

Then the Thing, running some red thread through the eye of a needle, concentrated on embroidering an ornate little monogram on some stiff Dutch linen, interlacing her own initials with those of How-Much-fer-Salt's.

With every passing day there was less and less air in the little white carriage, while her possessions breathed out their own redolence — persistent, corrosive, strong-smelling like cheap strawberry soap.

How-Much-fer-Salt's cheeks grew rounder, while the tiny, soft knob of his nose turned pink and greasy, befitting those of high rank.

52

Esenin had practically moved into the house on Prechistenka.

Isadora gave him a gold watch. She imagined that a watch would keep him from always rushing off, running away from her Empire armchairs to his mysterious appointments and unknown affairs.

Sergei Konyonkov divided all of humanity into those who wore watches and those who didn't.

Describing someone, he would usually mutter:

'This one ... wears a watch.'

We already knew that if it was an artist he was talking about, there was no point in debating his talents any further.

Now, as capricious fate would have it, the very epitome of the 'watchless man', Esenin, had a timepiece in his pocket, a gold, double-lidded Bouret watch, no less.

On top of that, whenever he met someone new, he would take the watch out of his pocket, and casually snap open the heavy gold lid, apparently just interested in the time.

In all other respects, the watch had not played its intended role. He went on running away from those soft armchairs to his unknown affairs and mysterious, non-existent appointments.

Sometimes he'd turn up at our place on Bogoslovky with a small parcel.

On such days he was serious and firm. The words rang out:

'Finally... I told her, "Isadora, *adieu*!" Like that.'

The small parcel generally contained two or three shirts, underpants and socks. Esenin's possessions were returning to Bogoslovsky.

We would smile.

I'd tell Kozhebatkin at the bookshop:

'Today Esenin told Isadora again, '*Adieu*! *Adieu*! Gimme my laundry.'

Two hours after Esenin's arrival from Prechistenka, the porter would come by with a letter. Esenin would pen a terse and inflexible reply.

Another hour, and Isadora's secretary, Ilya Ilyich Shneider, would be pressing our diminutive doorbell.

Finally, towards evening, Isadora herself would appear. Her lips swollen like a child's and those blue faience saucers glistening with salty tears.

She would drop onto the floor by Esenin's chair, embrace his leg, bestrew the red honey of her hair along his knees:

'Angel.'

Esenin would push her rudely her away with his boot.

'You go to...' he would lash her with coarse abuse.

Isadora, smiling more and more tenderly:

'Sergei Alexandrovich, I love you.'

It ended the same way every time.

Emilia would again bundle Esenin's belongings together in a parcel.

53

In the summer I saw Anna at least once every day.

After she returned from Kiev, I saw her twice every day. Then three times. It never felt like enough.

Then she finally wound up 'forevermore' in my small Bogoslovsky chamber.

It all happened quite simply: one evening I held her back and in the morning begged her not to leave.

'All the same you'll be rushing back to see me in an hour,' I said. 'It's not worth it.'

Anna agreed.

Two days later she brought to Bogoslovsky her little lace brassiere with pink ribbons. Her only possession.

54

Spring. Sunshine creeps in through the open window, along with a kind of naive, silly joy.

I'm trying to tighten the strap on a wildly over-stuffed suitcase.

But for all I huff and puff, as hard as my knee presses down on its yellow, imitation-leather paunch the valise won't cooperate.

I sit Anna down on top of the suitcase.

'Try to concentrate your weight.'

Light as a feather, she stuffs herself with air and laughter.

'One — two — THREE!'

Her blown-out cheeks release their load, the strap flies out of my hand, and the furious suitcase tosses its 'weight' upwards.

Esenin and Isadora sweep in.

Esenin is wearing a white silk muffler and white gloves, and carrying a little bunch of lovely spring flowers.

He supports Isadora's arm ceremoniously.

She is wearing a checked English suit and small hat, and smiles, looking younger.

Esenin hands his little bouquet to Anna.

Our train to the Caucuses leaves in an hour. Esenin's flight for Königsberg is in three days.

'And for you, my little dummyberry, I wrote some verse.'

'And I for you, Vyatka.'

Esenin recites his poem, investing the warm and sorrowful words with his warm and sorrowful voice:

PARTING WITH MARIENGOF

There's an unbridled joy in friendship,
A paroxysm of tempestuous feelings
When a fire is melting the body
As if it were a stearin candle.

Give me your hands, beloved —
I know no other way —
I want you to dip them, in this hour of parting,
In my head's yellow spume.

Oh, Tolya, Tolya, is it really you,
As countless times before
The circles of unmoving milky eyes
Grow still once more.

Farewell, farewell! In moonflames
Will I see again that joyous day?
Among the exalted and the young
You were the best of all for me.

Some day, some year,
We'll meet again, perhaps.
I'm scared: my soul is slipping away,
Like youth and like love.

Another will drown me in you.
Isn't it why, in harmony with my words,
My sobbing ears,
Lap like oars against my shoulders?

Farewell, farewell! In moonflames
I won't see that joyous day,
But among the vibrant and the young
You were the best of all for me.

See the Russian original of this poem on p.178

My own *Parting with Esenin* ends with the following lines:

And what if
When we meet again
One hand holding another grows cold
And a kiss of greeting breaks off.

55

Here is what Esenin wrote from abroad:

Ostende. July 9, 1922.

My sweet Tolya,

Here I thought you were passing the time in some land of melons and nasty fevers, like our marvelous trip in 1920, and now I learn from Ilya Ilyich's letter that you're in Moscow. My dear, my closest, most darling and best, I so wish to be out of here, away from this nightmarish Europe, to return to Russia, to our old hooliganism and youthful passions. There's such boredom here, and their Severyaninesque life is so meaningless.

Igor Severyanin (1887-1941) poet of the Ego-Futurist school, a pretentious aesthete he praised high-society values. Emigrated in 1918.

Right now I'm in Ostende: the unbelievably rancid North Sea and the swinish, vacant mugs of the Europeans. Due to the abundance of wines in these parts I've given up drinking and sip only seltzer. From Moscow it seemed to us that Europe was the vastest expanse for the dissemination of our ideas and poetry, but from here I can see: my God, how fabulous and bountiful is Russia in this regard. I don't think there's any other country like it, there can't be.

As for superficial impressions, after our rack and ruin, everything here looks neat and pressed. You would like the look of it at first, but later I think even you would start slapping your knee and whimpering like a dog. It's one big graveyard. All these people scurrying about quicker than lizards — they're not people, but graveyard worms. Their houses are coffins, their continent a crypt. Those who lived here died long ago, and only we remember them, since the worms can't.

Esenin was obviously experiencing a cultural shock during his first contact with the West.

My one purpose here is to publish the translations of two booklets (32 pages each) by two unfortunate authors whom few here know — and those who do are in literary circles. I'll publish them in English and French.

The 'two unfortunate authors' are Esenin and Mariengof. These projects never materialized. In 1922, there was a French edition of Esenin's *Confessions of a Hooligan*.

In Berlin I caused a great deal of scandal and commotion to be sure. My top hat and wide coat, made by a Berlin tailor, drove everyone mad. Everybody thinks I came here on Bolshevik money, as a Cheka man or an agitator. I find all this ridiculous and amusing. I sold my book to Grzhebin. They shy away from your books. I managed to sell my 'good book of poetry' only as a collection of new verse, yours and mine. Anyway, to hell with them, since they've all grown rotten here after five years of emigre life. Those who live in a crypt stink of carrion. If you want to make your way here, badger Ilya Ilyich; I'll write him about it specially. Only after

Grzhebin was a Russian-language publisher in Berlin.

everything I've seen here, I'm not crazy about you leaving Russia. We can't be entrusting our literary ground to other sentries. If you have a chance, of course, come if you like, but I'll tell you honestly: if I'm not out of here in a month, it'll be a miracle. It'll mean I do have that diabolical restraint in me that Kogan denies. I've been thinking of Turkestan. How wonderful it all was, good God! Right now I even love myself drunk, with all my scandals:

Sweet Tolya, greetings, greetings.

Your Sergei

My dear dummyberry.

I have deigned to send your swineness a dozen letters, while your swineness sends not a word.

Thus, I begin:

Dear sir, know you Europe? No. You know not Europe. My God, what an impression, how my heart beats... Oh, no, you know Europe not.

In the first place, good God, such filth, monotony, such spiritual poverty it turns your stomach. My heart beats, beats with the most desperate hatred. It itches so but there's nothing to scratch it with, to my sorrow — this is what a certain wonderful (though hateful in this instance) poet Erdman says. Why 'nothing'? I'm prepared, for this purpose, to stick a shoe brush down my throat, but my mouth is too small and my throat too narrow. Yes, he's right, this damned Erdman — kiss him a thousand times for me.

Nikolai Erdman (1902-1970) dramatist and poet. Exiled to Siberia for his political parables.

Yes, my dear carrot-top, yes. I've also written Sashka, and Zlaty — and from you, 'not a blessed word.'

Now I understand it all,
I'm no longer the boy I used to be:
In his constant search and anguish
A poet cannot love.

V.Sh. — Vadim Shershenevich (see p.13)

V. Sh. said that. In English his name is W. Shakespeare.

Oh, I realize now what rascals you are, and next time, in revenge, I'll write in English, so you won't understand a thing.

And so, just because you revolt me, just because you don't remember me, it is with an especially malicious delight that I had your scandalous poems translated into English and French, and am publishing them in Paris and London. In September I'll send all this to you, as soon as the books come out.

My address (for when you don't write):

S. Esenin

He wrote to Sakharov from Dusseldorf.

My dears. My good friends,

What can I tell you about this most horrible kingdom of philistinism bordering on imbecility? Besides the foxtrot, there's practically nothing here; they stuff themselves full of food and drink and then they foxtrot again. I've yet to meet a human being, and don't know where to look for one. Mr. Dollar is terribly in vogue, and to hell with art; its highest expression is the 'music hall.' I didn't even want to publish my books here, despite the affordability of paper and translators. Nobody cares about poetry. If the book market is Europe, and the critic is Lvov-Rogachevsky, then it's senseless, isn't it, to write verse to please them, to suit their tastes.

Here everything is pressed smooth, licked clean and combed flat like Mariengof's hair. The birds perch only where they're allowed. Well, where do we fit in with our indecent poetry? It's discourteous, you know, just like communism. At times I want to send all this to the devil and flee back home.

Even if we're poor, even if we have famine, cold and cannibalism, for all that we have a soul, something they've leased out here as undesirable, on the security of Smerdyakovism.

Smerdyakov: the evil-exploiting bastard son in Dostoyevsky's *The Brothers Karamazov.*

Of course, in some places they know about us, some of our poetry, mine and Tolya's has been translated — but what does it matter, when no one reads it?

Right now on my table there's an English journal with Anatoly's verse, which I don't even feel like sending him. It's a very good edition, but on the cover it says: printrun: 500 copies. This is the largest they have here.

Start up, my stallions! My coachman, carry me off! Dear mother, have pity on your poor son? You know: the Algerian bey has a big wart right under his nose! Tell all this to Klychkov and Startsev when they start cursing me. My soul will feel lighter.

Your Sergei

56

My friend Vladimir Sokolov, once an actor at the Kamerny Theater, now at the Max Reinhard theater in Berlin, staged a production of Dostoyevsky's *The Idiot* in German, with famous German actors. This was in the fall of 1925.

I was sitting on the Kurfurstendamm behind a tankard of Munich ale, waiting for Sokolov. A German Social-Democrat was sitting next to me. His lips were gray and thin, like a piece of cord.

'The Russians in Berlin love to tell a joke about us Germans,' he said. 'You've probably heard it: There's a revolutionary uprising going on in some town. They're in the midst of capturing the railway station, rushing up and down the halls. A Russian runs up to them and screams, "Why don't you go out onto the railway and capture the platform?" The Germans answer, "The ticket office is closed ... They're not issuing any platform tickets." '

I laughed and thought: they'd hardly tell a joke like that about us.

My companion supposed 'platform tickets' to be proof that the Germans would arrive at Socialism before anyone else, and by the shortest and most peaceful route.

Sokolov came in, sullen, angry.

'You know, I think I'll drop everything,' he grumbled. 'I can't ... It's as if they're doing it all out of spite. Look here, I was reading them the first act of *The Idiot.* You remember, when Rogozhin's telling Prince Myshkin about spending a night passed out on a street in Pskov and being gnawed by dogs. I had just read it, and suddenly — there's laughter ... I asked them, "What is it?" The actors glanced uneasily at one another. Then one of them said, "Herr Sokolow, this part's badly translated. It's not plausible. Dostoevsky couldn't have written that." "Well, what couldn't he have written?" "There, that part about the dogs biting him. It's completely impossible. The audience will laugh." "But what's there to laugh about?" — and I was starting to get angry. "How on earth," he replied, "can dogs bite people if they're muzzled?" And you know, I didn't argue; I just threw up my hands. We had to cut that part.'

When I think of Esenin in the West, that first little joke and Sokolov's story always spring to mind. Esenin felt himself, his inner world and his verse to be implausible and doomed to be deleted, like that dog without a muzzle that bit Rogozhin.

In the Kuban steppes the iron horse had already made Esenin wary. But how lowly and paltry it seemed compared to that Iron Steed, rumbling along on the other side of the globe.

In 1924 I was in Paris. I spent an entire day wandering about Versailles with Kusikov in the park and the Trianon palaces. We were drunk with exhaustion.

We had dinner not far from Versailles in a little restaurant. In the course of our conversation I told Kusikov:

'You know, Sandro, I was really angry once when I read in some Frenchman's novel that "Two Parisian bon vivants and two courtesans expend more wit and grace in one night than do the English, the French, the Russians and the Americans combined in one year." But now...'

'Sandro' — Alexander Kusikov. See p. 32

Without finishing my thought, I drank a large glass of cold white wine to Versailles, to the French, to Gallic genius.

Kusikov smiled:

'I don't think I ever told you, Anatoly, about my trip here with Esenin last year. I worked on him for a week. Finally talked him into it. We set out... Made it as far as this very restaurant... Here Esenin announced that he was famished. We sat down to breakfast, Esenin started drinking, got angry, kept on drinking and being angry...Until dark... And at night we headed back to Paris, without even a glimpse of Versailles; in the morning, sober, he applauded himself on his cunning and subterfuge. That's how he traversed all of Europe and America — like a blind man, not wishing to see or know anything.'

I recalled a passage from a letter Esenin had written long before, about how travel would be his ruin.

'I don't know,' he'd written, 'what I'd do if by some accident I was forced to circle the entire globe. I would need if not a pistol then something to destroy any sense of global dimensions.'

Nikolai Leskov (1831-95) Russian writer.

The Russo-French War of 1812 ended with Napoleon's defeat by the Russian army.

In one of Leskov's novels, an old woman who had served Prince Protozanov, Olga Fedotovna, finds herself abroad shortly after Alexander I's capture of Paris, in which her master had taken part. Upon his return to Russia, an embassy sacristan reports of Olga Fedotovna:

'She started all this as soon as we crossed the Rhine. She'd see some ruins, and go into raptures and start badgering everybody, "Look, dear sir, look, my lord caused all this devastation," and cry for joy.'

Pressing on with her theory on the destruction of all European buildings, in Paris she argued with the French servants, trying to convince them that the then-unfinished Notre Dame wasn't at all 'unfinished'; rather her lord had 'caused its devastation.'

When Princess Protozanov took the side of the scandalized French, Olga Fedotovna declared that she had no respect for her own family.

The time has come for us to admit that the patriotism which seized us during the years of War Communism bore much resemblance to Olga Fedotovna's ideological excesses.

Even the virtuoso obscurantism of Vasily Rozanov touched a chord in us — Rozanov proclaimed that it was no great achievement to love a happy and powerful motherland; that we should be able to love her when she was weak, small, humiliated, ignorant and even depraved. It was when our 'mother' was drunk, he maintained, when she told untruths and wallowed in sin, that we should love her most. But that wasn't all: when she finally died, leaving behind only bones 'gnawed clean by Jews' — a true Russian would be crying over her skeleton, worthless and spat on by all.

Vasily Rozanov (1856-1919) Russian philosopher and writer whose very distinctive style influenced many authors of his time, including Mariengof.

Esenin was savvy enough, when he found himself in Europe, to know how outmoded, decrepit, patchy, frayed and worn-through such convictions were — but he also lacked determinaton and courage to reject them, to find a new inner world.

57

Anna and I went off to the Black Sea for the summer. Our money ran out in August. Just then a bright-eyed vendor, brown as a clay figurine, barefoot and bare-bellied, began bawling morning, noon and night:

I got me here
In my little basket
All sorts of tidbits
Like in a Berlin store.

Fortunately, other peddlers had fewer temptations:

Cherries, cherries, two kopecks a pound...

And five-kopeck melons, sold by a serenading black-braided signora:

Meluns! Meluns!
Eat them quickly!
They's almost smokin'!

made the course of our days a bit less gloomy.

We filled our hollow stomachs with the bounty of the South, and wrote to friends in Moscow (that they might see about a small advance for me from some soft-hearted editor) and to our relations (that they might scrape together a small short-term loan).

Although, in all honesty, the chances of happening on a magnanimous editor or a solvent relative seemed to me equally slim.

Incidentally, I had practically no relatives (except for my sister) in the whole wide world. Our nearest relations were maybe grandmothers who dried their stockings under the same sun — that, I believe, is how good writers of old used to put it.

Then suddenly: a wire transfer for one hundred rubles arrived and all the bitterness evaporated from our souls. We even decided to gambol in the waves an extra week.

Over lunch we racked our brains: who could have sent us such a gift of plenty?

In the evening the postman handed us the answer to the riddle. A telegram:

'Arrived. Come. Esenin.'

Ecstatic, I started jumping up and down and clapping my hands.

My six-week-old son Kirill cast a shaming glance at me from the yellow leather toilet-case that served him as a cradle:

'Such a big Daddy but he jumps like a goat!'

Conscience-stricken, I waved a finger at his little pink pea-nose with its two little holes:

'Well, Kirill, old man, we're headed for Moscow. My only friend's come back from the insufferable Americas. Understand?'

The little pink pea-nose wrinkled up and sneezed.

'So it's true!'

In the morning Kirill swapped apartments — the leather toilet-case for a wooden washtub — and set out for Moscow on an express train.

58

'Here I am!'

'Vyatka!'

What a European! What a marvelous, splendid European! Look at that: even the shining tip of a fountain pen sticking out of the small pocket on his soft gray jacket.

His step seems even lighter in those pretentious white shoes, his hair still more golden from under the brim of his beautiful expensive hat the color of coffee with cream.

Only his eyes ... I don't understand... Odd — they're not his eyes.

'It's trash!'

'Hm?'

'Europe is trash.'

'Trash?'

'In Chicago you can stand on your tiptoes and reach the overhead rail line! Nonsense!'

And he raised himself contemptuously on the white toes of his pompous shoes.

'... In Venice the architecture isn't bad. But it sti-i-i-nks!' He wrinkled up his nose in the funniest way. 'In New York what I liked more than anything was this monkey that a banker had. The little stinker walked around in silk pajamas, smoked cigars and pestered the housemaids. And in Paris ... I was sitting in a bar... A garcon walked up... He said: "You, Esenin, may deign to eat here, but we, officers of the guard, have to work here with napkins over our arms..." "You're a waiter?" I asked him. "Yes!" "In that case," I told him, "shut up and bring me some champagne!" So there! Anyway, I had your poems translated, published my book in French... But it was all pointless. No one there cares about poetry. And as for Isadora — adieu!'

'Gimme my laundry?'

'No, no, adieu forever ... Forever ... I'm Russian ... and she's ... I ... I can't ... You know, when I crossed the border — I wept ... I kissed the earth ... Like some Ryazan peasant woman ... Shall I read you some verse?'

He recited all of *Moscow of the Taverns* and *The Black Man*.

'*Moscow of the Taverns* is beautiful,' I told him. 'Your verse has never had such lyrical power, such tragedy. You've managed to raise the Gypsy romance form to the level of high, very high art. But *The Black Man* is terrible. Really terrible. It's no good at all.'

'But Gorky cried. I read it to him. He cried real tears...'

Maxim Gorky (1868-1936) the first really major Russian wrter to emerge from the proletariat. Lived abroad from 1921 to 1928.

'I don't know...'

Esenin didn't submit *The Black Man* for publication and never read it again until his very last days when, as I recall, he made some fairly negligible revisions.

That evening we went out to some bohemian tavern on Nikitskaya, either The Stray Dog or The Rambling Enthusiast.

Esenin was drunk after the first glass of wine. He caused a bitter and dismal scene: he punched somebody, cursed, smashed dishes, overturned tables, ripped up his money and flung it into the air. He looked at me with glazed, unseeing eyes that didn't recognize me. Only one word registered: Kirill.

'Seryozha, you'll frighten Kirill,' Anna told him. 'Don't drink any more ... He's a baby... You can't behave like that around him...'

Esenin quieted down for a minute.

That same magic word led him out of the tavern.

In the cab on the way home Esenin dropped his head on my shoulder as if it weren't his, as if it were superfluous, a cold bony sphere.

With a stranger's help, I lugged his heavy, brittle and uncooperative body into the room on Bogoslovsky. The sunken whites of his eyes shone out from under deathly sallow lids. There was saliva on his lips, as if he'd just eaten a pastry (greedily, slovenly) and sullied his mouth with the sweet, sticky cream. His cheeks and forehead were deathly white, like a sheet of Whatman paper.

Such was our reunion. From morning till night.

I could not get his poem about *The Black Man* out of my mind.

I was unnerved. Maybe Gorky had been right to cry.

59

The next day Esenin brought his American wardrobe-trunks over to Bogoslovsky. They were large, yellow, tied together with hoops; inside they contained shelves, drawers and clothes hooks. Black porters would throw such trunks down onto cement and asphalt practically from the third floor without thinking.

Inside the trunks were a dozen jackets, silk underwear, a tuxedo, a top hat, other hats, a mantle for a tail coat.

Esenin was scared to death; he suspected every one of either already having robbed him or planning to.

He would check the locks on the trunks several times a day. When stepping out, he'd whisper furtively in my ear:

'Keep an eye on them, Tolya! Not a living soul — nobody! — is to come into this room. I know them — they go around with lock-picks in their pockets.'

He thought he saw his socks and ties on other poets, on friends and acquaintances. When greeting people he'd sniff them to see if they smelled of his cologne.

This was neither imbecility nor stinginess.

I recall that first night, the foam on his lips like sweet cream, the stranger's eyes in that dear, familiar face — and how he ripped money and scattered it around.

It wasn't like that before.

Once Meyerhold and Zinaida Raikh were over for pancakes. We drank vodka with the pancakes. Esenin more than anyone else. He became raucous and started smashing dishes. I whispered in his ear:

'Stop it, Seryozha. We barely have any crockery, and here you are breaking the little that we have.'

When Meyerhold wasn't looking Esenin winked at me archly, nodded his head reassuringly and pointed to a plate lying on the floor, unbroken.

It was child's play from there. On the table, besides a little porcelain service, there was an enameled plate. This he threw on the floor, producing a bang and crash; then he deftly and inconspicuously picked it up, replaced it on the table and sent it flying once more.

Or take the time when our white Turkestan train carriage was standing on a siding in Rostov.

A drunken Esenin came back from town. He started making a scene. The conductor stuck his head out the carriage window and announced:

'Comrade Molabukh ordered me not to let you in the carriage, Sergei Alexandrovich, not in this'n state!'

'Me? Not let me in?'

'He ordered me not to, Sergei Alexandrovich, sir!'

'You better lemme in!'

'It's against orders.'

'Tell your boss if he doesn't lemme in I'll smash up his shack!'

'It's against orders.'

At that point Esenin, wheezing, began smashing in the carriage windows.

Glass fell tinkling onto the sleepers. A pale How-Much-fer-Salt stood in his compartment in his undershirt and drawers, a candle in his trembling hand.

Esenin wouldn't stop.

Even three days after the havoc How-Much-fer-Salt still refused to make up with Esenin. To all my inducements he answered:

'What're you tellin' me, "He was drunk! Drunk! He wasn't himself!" Uh-uh, brother, he was very much himself. He's always himself. When he was bangin' on my glass, he kept his hand inside his sleeve just so's he wouldn't cut himself, God forbid. And you with your "He was drunk! He wasn't himself!" He smashed all my windows — and not one scratch on his little finger. He's a sly one, brother. And you with your "Drunk ... Not himself..." '

That was Esenin.

If on the day of our first meeting in The Stray Dog he'd shown bills but torn up plain paper, I would have known that despite his sunken lids, the cream-like foam on his lips and the apathetic, brittle body, things weren't all that bad.

60

The sorrow foreseen in our *Partings* turned real and distinct.

First our literary paths began to diverge.

Esenin was still publishing his verse in the Imagist journal *Inn for Travelers in the Beautiful*, but already he was looking in the direction of the peasant poets. He'd sit with Oreshin, Klychkov, and Shiryayevets in a little basement room of the Pegasus' Stall, arguing, shouting, drinking.

Oreshin, see p.23

Klychkov, see p. 88

Esenin wanted to run the journal they were planning, *Russians*. He demanded: 'Dictatorship!'

Oreshin angrily and ominously showed him a thumb between two fingers. Klychkov, his eyes narrow with spite, hated him with a heavy envious hate.

Alexander Shiryayevets (1887-1924) peasant poet.

Esenin went off to Petersburg and returned with Nikolai Klyuev, who embraced his literary little brothers like a pastor, kissed them thrice on the lips, called Esenin 'Seryozha' and even rubbed my knee tenderly, saying 'A deer! A deer!'

Klyuev, see p.20

He pined for his Olonets log house and languished every day, until closing time, until four in the morning, in Pegasus' Stall, among the violins squealing out foxtrots and the red-lipped, cold-hearted, foul-mouthed crowds reeking of wine, cheap 'Leda' powder and the turbid, petty passions of Tverskoi Boulevard.

I liked Klyuev. I even liked the way he'd make the sign of the cross over his watery beer and smoked fish, and the way he'd wear a crown of thorns, standing in a cathedral parvis among the beggars, his hand outstretched, his heart cynical and blasphemous and cold to love and faith, and all that for the sake of the mystic masquerade and great lie we call art.

Esenin was affectionate and obsequious towards Klyuev. He told him about *Russians* while turning over in his head how to enlist Big Brother's support for his 'dictatorship,' and to use him to reconcile Klychkov and Oreshin.

Meanwhile, Klyuev sighed:

'You know, Seryozha, soon I'll have to wear bast sandals. My last pair of shoes has fallen all to pieces.'

Esenin immediately ordered a pair of kid leather shoes for Klyuev.

In Pegasus' Stall that evening he kept pressing:

'Well, what about *Russians*, Nikolai?'

'Sure, sure, Seryozha. You're in charge. The Red Corner's yours.'

'You tell Klychkov and Oreshin, tell 'em, "It's Esenin's dictatorship." '

'I'll tell them, Seryozha, I'll tell them...'

The shoes would take a whole week to make.

Klyuev upbraided Esenin:

'Why'd you ever go and leave Isadora? She was a good woman... Rich... Now if only I had her... I'd buy myself a plush hat and I'd have a frock coat made from priests' cloth.'

'We'll get it for you, Nikolai, we'll get it! But about *Russians*...'

When the kid leather shoes were ready, Klyuev wrapped them up in a small knapsack and that very night, very quietly, without saying goodbye to anyone, he slipped out of Moscow.

61

Just as Esenin and I had begun to drift apart as poets, so we began to drift apart as friends.

I had recently returned from Paris and was sitting in our cafe, listening to the doleful wail of a thick double-bass string. The place was almost deserted not counting one young waitress with an abcessed tooth and another who hadn't even bothered to put on lipstick. What on earth was going on?

Outside it was dismal weather: sleet punctuated by the jaundiced, feeble glow of a street lamp.

How pleasant it would be, I mused, to ward off this autumnal misery with some merry Montparnasse songs... when who should walk in but Esenin. The young lady with the abscess and the other one with unrouged lips recoiled in fright. Esenin's eyes were lackluster and porous like a sugar cube dropped in a cup of hot coffee. His clothes were a shambles. His hat was stained and crushed, his collar limp and his tie askew. The golden foam of his hair was dishevelled and grayish, starting to look like the dirty water left in a washtub after a load of laundry.

Esenin, without saying hello, walked up to my table. He put his hands in his pockets and, uttering not a word, fixed me with his glazed, inimical stare.

We hadn't seen each other in several months. When leaving Russia, I hadn't had a chance to say goodbye. But there was no quarrel between us. It was just that our relationship had cooled.

I kept stirring my coffee with a spoon and stared silently back at him.

Some minor Petersburg poet was fussing over him. A woman walked up to Esenin and started pulling him by the sleeve.

'Fuck off! Can't you see I've run into Mariengo-o-of here...'

Esenin reeked of alcohol, acrid and vile:

'Well?'

He let his hands fall heavily onto the table, bent down, and, his face almost jammed against mine, rapped out each syllable:

'I'll devour you!'

He meant this in a literary sense.

'You're not the Big Bad Wolf, and I'm not Little Red Riding Hood. So maybe you won't.'

I squeezed out a smile, raised my cup and swallowed some hot coffee.

'No ... I will!'

Esenin made a fist.

The Petersburg poet (puny, morose, with a nose like an exclamation point) and the unknown woman tried, in whispers, to prevail upon Esenin and to convince me of something.

Esenin straightened up, put his hands back in his pockets, turned on his heels and staggered unsteadily towards the door.

The poet and the woman each took an arm. At the door, Esenin spun his head round as if it were on a screw and doffed his hat:

'Adieu!'

He furiously worked his jaws.

'All the same ... I will!'

The little poet opened the door for him.

That was our whole quarrel. The first in six years. In a month we'd be running into each other on the street and looking the other way.

62

In the spring Anna and I went abroad once more, and again we returned to Moscow in the thick of late October's gloom and sleet. On one of our first days back we called on the Kachalovs. In their tiny apartment on Kamergersky they treated us to some nice wine.

Kachalov read some verse — Blok, Esenin. In a corner, its short black fur and large intelligent eyes glimmering, sat Kachalov's Doberman pinscher. Kachalov petted its perfect pointed muzzle.

Vasily Kachalov, leading actor at the Maly drama theater.

'Jim ... Isn't Jim a beauty?'

'He certainly is.'

'Esenin wrote a poem about him!'

Kachalov recited the poem dedicated to Jim.

Afterwards I asked:

'How is Esenin? Are things going well for him, or poorly?'

Our enmity had filled our souls with all sorts of muck. It was as if we were carrying slop-pails around inside ourselves.

But time had overturned even those slop-pails, and wiped them out with a wet rag. In a word, they were clean, clean as a whistle.

'They're not going at all well.'

Kachalov told me, in very sympathetic terms, what he'd noticed during their occasional meetings, what he'd heard through the grapevine and from people who were close to Esenin or saw him.

'Where's Seryozha now? Everything turned out so stupidly between us. For no reason and to no good...'

We stayed in that tiny room till late. Upon leaving, I said:

'As soon as I find out where he's hanging around I'll go and make up with Esenin.'

That very night Esenin had been at our place on Bogoslovsky, for several hours awaiting our return. He'd tucked up our son Kirill in his little bed, hummed him a lullaby and chatted with my drowsy mother-in-law about life, eternity, poetry, friendship and love.

Finally tired of waiting, he'd left before we got home.

'Tell them I came by,' he'd said, 'with open arms, in peace, tell them...'

I didn't sleep all night. My unbidden tears wet the pillow.

The next morning I ran all over the city asking around where Esenin was living.

Those who might have known just spread their hands in a gesture of ignorance.

But that evening, as I was swallowing some cold soup, the doorbell rang in a way I recognized instantly — although I hadn't heard it for some 500 days, if not more.

It was Esenin.

63

About a week passed.

I had been bustling about in pursuit of The Ruble. All bustled out, I came home.

Anna opened the door:

'Seryozha's here...' She added in alarm: 'He brought some wine ... He's drinking...'

Whenever she said, 'Esenin's drinking,' the words would clatter like a crutch.

I walked into the room.

That jaundiced glaze from the bottle hadn't yet flowed into his eyes.

We kissed tenderly.

'The Marmoset was rude to me just now...' Esenin archly stuck out his lip: 'She doesn't want to join me in a drink ... To our truce. To our love for each other...'

He poured himself some flat champagne.

'Let's wait a bit, Sergei ... We'll have a bite first ... Marmoset'll give us some nice cabbage soup with black oats.'

Esenin raised his eyebrows.

'I don't eat much these days ... I hardly eat at all...'

He drank down the wine in one gulp.

'I'm gonna die in the spring. Ah, come on, don't get all worked up. I tell you I'm gonna die, so there, that's it.'

Again those guileful lips:

'I've got ... consumption of the larynx ... So: it's the end!'

I started talking about Italy, about how we'd go off together in the spring to the warm Adriatic, lie on the hot sand, drink something better than this vile stuff (I put the bottle under the table), and luxuriate in the flaring, marvelous melted gold of D'Annunzio's sun.

Gabriele D'Annunzio (1863-1938) Italian poet, novellist, playwright.

'No, I'm gonna die.'

He said the word 'die' with firm decision, and enviable equanimity.

I wanted to howl, to curse him, to scrape my nails on the cold, slippery wood of the armchair.

Watery salt gnawed at my eyes.

Anna was looking for something on the floor, taking her time, afraid to raise her head.

Later Esenin recited a poem about vanished youth and the tremors of the grave, which he promised to accept as a new caress.

64

'Whom are you here to see?'

'Esenin.'

The duty physician writes me out a pass.

I go up some silent, carpeted stairs. A large room. The walls are painted in soft, warm colors. The blue peephole of a small electric lamp hangs from the ceiling.

Esenin sits up in bed, hugging his knees.

'Seryozha, your face looks fine. Your hair is even starting to fluff up again.'

It had been a long time since I'd seen Esenin with such clear eyes, such tranquil hands, eyebrows and mouth. The gray dust had fallen from his eyelids.

I recalled our last meeting:

Esenin had drunk a bottle of champagne to the last drop. The jaundiced glaze had poured into his eyes. On one wall hung a Ukrainian rug with large red and yellow flowers. Esenin had stared at them intently. The seconds had crept ominously by, while Esenin's pupils, their irises widening, had writhed and squirmed even more ominously. The whites of his eyes had filled with red and the tiny black holes of his pupils with a horrid, naked madness.

Esenin had stood up from the armchair, crumpled up his napkin and, handing it to me, wheezed in my ear:

'Wipe their noses!'

'Seryozha, it's just a rug... A rug... And these are flowers...'

The black holes flashed with hatred:

'Ah! You coward!'

He seized an empty bottle and gnashed his teeth:

'I'll smash them... their blood... their noses... blood... I'll smash...'

I took a napkin and started running it along the rug — wiping their red and yellow faces, blowing their noses.

Esenin wheezed.

My blood ran cold.

There is a lot that drowns in memory. But something like that — never.

And now: a little blue peephole in the ceiling. A narrow bed with a small gray blanket. Warm-colored walls. And his nearly-still hands, eyebrows, mouth.

'I quite like it here,' Esenin said. 'The only thing that bothers me a bit is that the little blue lamp is on night and day. You know, I wrap myself up in the blanket. I lie with my head under the pillow. And they don't let me close the door. They're all afraid I'll kill myself.'

Esenin's diagnosis was 'Delirium Tremens. Hallucinations.'

In the corridor a very pretty woman walked by: big, blue eyes and beautiful hair, like golden honey.

'Everyone wants to die here ... That Ophelia there hung herself by her hair.'

Later Esenin took me to the reception room. He showed me the chains and fetters in which they sometimes shackled the patients; their drawings, needlework and painted sculptures made of wax and the soft insides of bread loaves.

'Look at this, a painting by Vrubel. He was here too.'

Mikhail Vrubel (1856-1910) Symbolist painter, particularly famous for his series of paintings representing the Demon.

Esenin smiled:

'Just don't get it into your head that this is the looney bin. The looney bin's right near here, though.'

He led me to the window:

'There it is, that building!'

Through the snow-covered leaves of the December park, the illuminated windows of a hospitable manor house stared contentedly back at us.

65

Plato expelled Homer from his ideal republic for being indecent.

I am not Homer.

Ours is a republic of Soviets, not the ideal one.

May I say something indecent? Something just mildly indecent: about how to ask for happiness from life.

One should ask for happiness the way an Odessa tramp begs for money:

'Madam citizen, give us a fiver. If you don't I'll spit in your eye — and mind you I've got syphilis.'

66

A woman visiting a prison learned of her husband's death. She started to cry. A guard came up to her and said:

'Madam citizen, if you want to grieve, go outside.'

67

On 31 December 1925, Esenin's little hillock sprang up in Moscow's Vagankov cemetery.

In the last year of his life Esenin attempted suicide several times. On 28 December 1925 he hung himself in the Angleterre Hotel in Leningrad, having written his last poem in his own blood.

68

I recalled another December 31st: 'Ring In the New Year with the Imagists' at the Polytechnic Museum.' Esenin and I — young, happy. The evening public on Tverskaya Street is outraged by our effulgent top hats. The sleigh creaks. Our beaver collars shine silver with hoarfrost.

Esenin carries on a literary conversation with the cabman:

'Tell us, uncle: what poets do you know?'

'Pushkin.'

'That one's dead, uncle. C'mon, don't you know any live poets?'

'Not a blessed one, sir. We don't know any live ones. We only knows them cast-iron ones.'

1926

Мариенгоф

ПРОЩАНИЕ С МАРИЕНГОФОМ

Есть в дружбе счастье оголтелое
И судорога буйных чувств —
Огонь растапливает тело,
Как стеариновую свечу.

Возлюбленный мой, дай мне руки, —
Я по-иному не привык, —
Хочу омыть их в час разлуки
Я желтой пеной головы.

Ах, Толя, Толя, ты ли, ты ли,
В который миг, в который раз —
Опять, как молоко, застыли
Круги недвижущихся глаз.

Прощай, прощай! В пожарах лунных
Дождусь ли радостного дня?
Среди прославленных и юных
Ты был всех лучше для меня.

В такой-то срок, в таком-то годе,
Мы встретимся, быть может, вновь...
Мне страшно, — ведь душа проходит,
Как молодость и как любовь.

Другой в тебе меня заглушит.
Не потому ли — в лад речам
Мои рыдающие уши,
Как весла, плещут по плечам?

Прощай, прощай! В пожарах лунных
Не зреть мне радостного дня,
Но все ж средь трепетных и юных
Ты был всех лучше для меня.

The autograph of Esenin's last poem,
written in his own blood before he hanged himself

До свиданья, друг мой, до свиданья.
Милый мой, ты у меня в груди.
Предназначенное расставанье
Обещает встречу впереди.
До свиданья, друг мой, без руки, без слова,
Не грусти и не печаль бровей, —
В этой жизни умирать не ново,
Но и жить, конечно, не новей.
С. Е.

Farewell, my dear friend, farewell,
Within my heart you'll stay,
And as we part, I can foretell
That we shall meet some day.
Without a hand or a word, good-bye,
Don't mourn for me or grieve—
For it's not new for us to die,
Not newer still, to live.

Translated by Alexander Shaumyan

Anatoly Mariengof in the 1920s

Mariengof and Esenin. 1921

Sergei Esenin. 1924

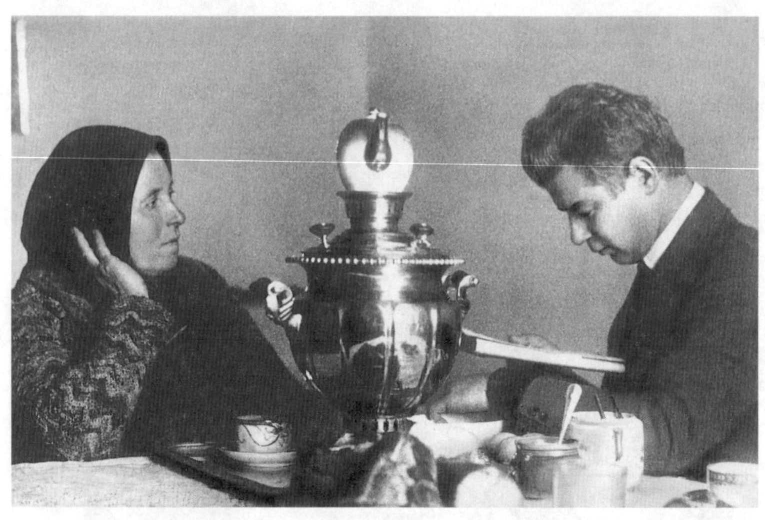

Esenin reading his poems to his mother in Konstantinovo. 1925

Esenin's mother. 1946

Esenin with his father and uncle. 1913

Esenin among villagers in Konstantinovo. 1909-10

Esenin in 1915

Esenin as an army recruit. 1916

Esenin and poet Nikolai Klyuev. 1916

Esenin and poet Sergei Gorodetsky. 1915

Sitting: Vadim Shershenevich and Esenin; standing: Mariengof's girlfriend Ellen Sherishevskaya, Mariengof, Ivan Gruzinov

From left to right: Mariengof, Esenin, Alexander Kusikov, Lev Povitsky

Esenin in 1925

Zinaida Raikh, Esenin's first wife

Isadora Duncan

Esenin and Duncan just married